Daily Blessings
for My
Secret Pal

Daily Blessings for My Secret Pal
ISBN 1-56292-910-0
Copyright © 2000 by GRQ Ink, Inc.
381 Riverside Drive, Suite 250
Franklin, Tennessee 37064

Published by Honor Books
P.O. Box 55388
Tulsa, Oklahoma 74155

Developed by GRQ Ink, Inc.
Manuscript written by Melody Carlson
Cover and text design by Richmond & Williams
Composition by Educational Publishing Concepts, Inc.

Daily Blessings for My Secret Pal

Devotions to
Share with
Your Special
Friend

Honor Books
Tulsa, Oklahoma

ℐ CALL UPON GOD,
AND THE LORD WILL
SAVE ME.

ℰVENING AND MORNING
AND AT NOON
ℐ UTTER MY COMPLAINT
AND MOAN,

AND HE WILL HEAR
MY VOICE.

PSALM 55:16-17 NRSV

*Blessings from
Your Secret Pal*

O Lord, *in the morning you hear my voice; in the morning I plead my case to you, and watch.*

PSALM 5:3 NRSV

This book is for you, dear friend, to tell you that you are special and that I am thinking about you. I hope that each blessing will be so rich and full that it will overflow to all those around you. I pray that as you read the Scriptures, you will become aware of God's love for you and His concern for the things that touch your life.

Through extraordinary days as well as ordinary ones, dear friend, I pray that you will rest in the comfort of these daily blessings. I pray that you will also be able to feel God's guiding and comforting hand in every circumstance.

Be glad today because you are not alone. God loves you—and I love you, too! Open your heart and let love flow freely to you from the pages of this book. And as your own special friend, I promise to pray for you. Take my hand now, and let us begin this amazing journey together!

Grace and peace in Him,

Your Secret Pal

God's Love

**I am like an olive tree growing in God's Temple. I trust God's
love forever and ever. God, I will thank you forever
for what you have done. With those who worship you,
I will trust you because you are good.**

PSALM 52:8-9 NCV

Dear Secret Pal,

God's love for you is immense and powerful. It is greater than any
love you have ever known before. Even if you don't yet know Him, He
still loves you. You can trust His amazing love. Again and again He
reaches out to you with loving arms of sweet compassion in the same way a
mother reaches for her child.

Open your heart today and embrace this divine love that has been given
to you by the very One who created you. Breathe in the deep peace and
abundant joy that comes with knowing your life has purpose and meaning.
Rest in His promise that He will never leave you nor forsake you.

Lord God, reveal Yourself to my secret pal. Let her feel the
magnitude of Your love for her and the strength of Your commitment to
her. Help her feel my love for her as well. Amen.

God's Sufficient Love

I love you, O LORD, my strength.
The LORD is my rock, my fortress, and my deliverer,
my God, my rock in whom I take refuge,
my shield, and the horn of my salvation, my stronghold.

PSALM 18:1-2 NRSV

Dear Secret Pal,

*A*s you awaken to the reality of God's love for you, I pray that you will begin to feel the joy and vitality this knowledge brings to your life. Everyday annoyances, problems large and small, will reveal themselves for what they truly are—temporary occurrences that diminish when put in the perspective of God's great love.

I pray that as you surrender your burdens and cares to Him, you will begin to feel a freedom that comes from knowing He is watching over you. He does hear us when we pray, and I can tell you that when I have reached out to Him, He has never once failed me. He will be just as faithful to you, as you learn to place your trust in Him.

*L*oving Father, I pray that as my secret pal reaches out to take Your hand, You will fill her with assurance and make her bold and confident in Your great love for her. Amen.

God's Goodness

This is the day that the LORD has made;
let us rejoice and be glad in it.

PSALM 118:24 NRSV

Dear Secret Pal,

A new day is like a unique treasure—a gift from Heaven. Each day is an opportunity to love God more and to experience His love for us. Even in the repetitious, everyday matters of life—going to the grocery store, carrying out simple tasks at work, cooking meals, interacting with family members—God is there.

If you look closely, you can see abundant evidence of this, for His simple gifts are everywhere—the light of a child's smile, the melody of a songbird, the whiff of a flower's fragrance, the sound of the wind in the trees overhead. All these whisper of God's glory and majesty when our hearts are tuned into His infinite goodness. The Lord created this new day. He has placed us, you and me, with all our hopes and fears, right in the middle of it. I plan to make the most of it. How about you?

Dear Lord, I pray that You will kindle an awareness of Your goodness in the heart of my secret pal. Open her eyes to see all the simple things in her life that You have freely given her. Amen.

Grateful Hearts

We give thanks to You, O God, we give thanks!
For Your wondrous works declare that Your name is near.

PSALM 75:1 NKJV

~⊙~

Dear Secret Pal,

I don't know about you, but I often find myself so busy working, commuting, meeting family demands, or even fixing a backed-up sink, that I forget to thank God for the good things in my life. Then I have to pause and ask Him to help me see things correctly again. I need His gentle nudge to improve my outlook, and that's when I start to realize how I've taken some beautiful blessings for granted.

A grateful heart doesn't always come naturally. It is an attitude, a state of mind, something you and I must choose daily. I know from experience, though, that it is well worth the effort. Why? Because it can change the way I view life. It can wash away resentment and leave me feeling refreshed and loved day after day. It can do the same for you, too.

———— ~⊙~ ————

*L*ord God, I pray that You will help my secret pal and me establish an attitude of thankfulness in our lives. Each day, give us fresh eyes to see Your goodness and love. Amen.

Pray without Ceasing

**To you, O LORD, I lift up my soul. . . .
for you are the God of my salvation;
for you I wait all day long.**

PSALM 25:1,5 NRSV

ᴄᴐᎧᎧᏼ

Dear Secret Pal,

What is the first thing you do when trouble comes knocking at your door? How do you handle really desperate situations, like grave illness, financial crisis, or personal loss? Do you pray and ask for God's help and strength? I do. In fact, most people cry out to God in times of need.

But God is present and willing to hear and help in ordinary times, as well as those dark and desperate places. Open your heart to God each day. Talk to Him about both big and little things in your life. Trust Him with your everyday cares and concerns. He wants you to feel His love in the good times as well as the bad.

ᴄᴐᎧᎧᏼ

Lord God, help my secret pal come to know You as Friend, as well as Helper and Defender. Open her heart to appreciate a day-to-day relationship with You. Amen.

Slowing Down

**Be still and know that I am God.
I will be exalted among the nations,
I will be exalted on the earth.**

PSALM 46:10 MLB

Dear Secret Pal,

*H*urrying seems to be part and parcel of our lives today. I find myself rushing from this to that, breathless and fearful that I'll be late for an appointment or that a project won't be completed on schedule or that my bills won't be paid on time. Do you find this to be true also? These things seem so important. And yet I know God does not want us to rush through our lives in a flurry of confusion.

Let's agree together. When we feel that hurried feeling pulling us into its grip, let's agree to ask God to help us slow down and put things in perspective. Let's set our hearts on Him and let Him show us those things that are really important.

*H*eavenly Father, I pray that You will establish Your stillness and truth in my heart and in the heart of my secret pal. Let our actions be a reflection of Your peace. Amen.

Abundant Living

**Let your heart keep my commandments;
for length of days and years of life
and abundant welfare they will give you.**

PROVERBS 3:1-2 NRSV

Dear Secret Pal,

*T*he secret to the good life—a life rich in blessings and peace—is found only in God. For He is the One who wants to lead and guide you. And like a loving father, He has wonderful things in store for you. His whole desire is to protect and guard you and to bless you with His presence. He has promised to walk with you through each day, if you will keep His commandments.

That sounds like an impossible task, I know. But Jesus said we can keep all of His commandments by living a life of love—to love God with all our hearts and souls and minds, and then to love others the way we love ourselves. So how is this love attainable? We must open our hearts; He will do the rest.

*L*ord God, help my secret pal and me as we endeavor to keep Your loving commandments. Fill us to overflowing that we might bless others with the same blessings You have poured out on us. Amen.

God's Deliverance from Fear

I sought the LORD, and He heard me,
And delivered me from all my fears.
They looked to Him and were radiant,
And their faces were not ashamed.

PSALM 34:4-5 NKJV

Dear Secret Pal,

Fear dwells all around us. Just open the newspaper or turn on the television, and there it is. But fear holds no more threat than a shadow when we place our trust in God. What wonderful freedom we have when we know that He is always watching over us—our able Defender. We are able to move through life with serene confidence when we're assured of God's protection and deliverance.

Give your fears to God today. In exchange, He will give you His peace and His promise to walk with you through every circumstance of life. God loves you! And He is faithful to watch over all those things you entrust to Him.

Dear God, I pray that You will deliver my secret pal and me from fear's grip. Give us courage to surrender our fears and place our trust in Your faithful and uplifting hand. Amen.

Everlasting Life

For God so loved the world,
that he gave his only begotten Son,
that whosoever believeth in him
should not perish, but have everlasting life.

JOHN 3:16 KJV

Dear Secret Pal,

Think of it—God has given the gift of eternal life to all who place their trust in Him. Though we did nothing to deserve His great love, He cared for us and reached out His hand to us. In essence, our eternal life begins the moment we entrust Him with our hearts. And God has much more in store for us. He not only guards and blesses our lives here on earth, but He also promises that He will always be with us, loving and caring for us, throughout eternity.

God loves us so dearly, so completely, that He wants us to be with Him always! What deep and profound joy this brings to our hearts—yet who can understand such things or even find words to describe such glory!

Heavenly Father, although it strains our imaginations to conceive of the gift of everlasting life that You have given us, we rejoice and praise You unceasingly for it. Amen.

God's Strength

The LORD is my strength and my shield;
My heart trusted in Him, and I am helped;
Therefore my heart greatly rejoices,
And with my song I will praise Him.

PSALM 28:7 NKJV

Dear Secret Pal,

*D*o you ever feel weak and overwhelmed? We all do from time to time. It's a part of our stressful, modern lifestyle. But God does not want us to live exhausted, defeated lives. When we feel weak, He wants to support us with His strength.

My problem is that I sometimes find it difficult to admit that I need God's help. I like to think that I can handle things on my own. However, I am learning to place my trust in Him at all times—those times when I feel weak and those times when I feel strong. I want to encourage you also to release yourself into His care today. Depend on Him. He will never let you down.

*L*ord God, when we depend on ourselves, we are weak; but when we depend on You, we are strong. Forgive us when we look within ourselves for the strength that only You can give us. Amen.

A Generous Heart

*Don't forget to do good
and to share what you have with those in need,
for such sacrifices are very pleasing to God.*

HEBREWS 13:16 NLT

Dear Secret Pal,

*W*hen we give of our time and resources to meet the needs of others, we are doing for them what God has done for us. He poured out His love on us, expecting nothing in return. And He continues to give us all that we need and so much more! Giving to others assures us that we are like our Father—we are truly His children.

Some people think it seems unreasonable to give when they barely have enough, but I have found that giving is like priming a pump—it gives us access to God's blessings. When we give from our hearts to others, God gives from His heart to us, and we can never outdo His overwhelming generosity. Try it and you'll see what I mean.

---

*A*lmighty God, thank You for Your infinite goodness to us. Give us the insight and ability to carry that goodness into the world, that we may bless others as You have blessed us. Amen.

Adoration of God

Sing to the Lord, O kingdoms of the earth—
sing praises to the Lord,
to him who rides upon the ancient heavens,
whose mighty voice thunders from the sky.

PSALM 68:32-33 TLB

Dear Secret Pal,

To truly know God is to adore Him. The warmth and light of His presence fills our hearts, and we can't help but erupt in praise and thanksgiving and adoration! Something truly amazing happens when we focus our praise and attention onto God. What an experience to be lifted out of ourselves to worship in His presence!

You may have discovered, as I have, that human relationships often carry an obligation of thankfulness, but God gives freely, allowing us to thank Him and praise Him freely. Let's pause to remember today all the blessings He has poured out on our lives and then open our hearts and our mouths to thank Him.

Lord God, Heavenly King, God the Father Almighty, we worship You, we give You thanks, we praise You for Your glory.

Grace

**For by grace are ye saved through faith;
and that not of yourselves: it is the gift of God:
Not of works, lest any man should boast.**

EPHESIANS 2:8-9 KJV

Dear Secret Pal,

Grace is God's unmerited favor, His unearned love, His undeserved forgiveness. He generously pours out this incredible grace simply because He loves us. When we come to God through faith, we begin to experience His grace. He pours out His grace on us because He loves us, not because we have earned His goodwill. Grace is the quiet power bestowed on us when we come to God through faith.

With grace we are capable of anything and everything good. It supplies us with that superhuman spark of divine love that God plants in our hearts. In fact, it is only through His grace that we can reach out to others with love and compassion. Let's open our hearts to receive His grace today.

Sweet Father God, we are glad to be Your children. I pray that You will continue to shower Your grace on my secret pal and me as we come before You with thankful and expectant hearts. Amen.

Mercy

**Through the LORD's mercies we are not consumed,
Because His compassions fail not.
They are new every morning.**

LAMENTATIONS 3:22-23 NKJV

✦

Dear Secret Pal,

*M*ercy is a precious commodity and a deeply imbedded part of our relationship with God and with each other. And like a crystal-clear, freshwater lake, fed by a clean stream and later flowing into a bubbling brook, mercy is something that we must give and receive on a daily basis to remain healthy.

Let's choose to practice mercy today, dear friend, by forgiving others' mistakes, by showing kindness and compassion to those around us. And then we can lift our hands and open our hearts and be washed anew in God's tender mercies. And like the bright and sparkling morning, we, too, can be made fresh and clean!

✦

*L*ord God, help my secret pal and me as we strive to practice mercy. Give us hearts that are tender to the needs of those around us. Amen.

The Kingdom of God

**The Kingdom of God isn't ushered in with visible signs.
You won't be able to say, "It has begun here in this place or
there. . . ." For the Kingdom of God is within you.**

LUKE 17:20-21 TLB

∽◎◎◠

Dear Secret Pal,

God's kingdom has come. Indeed, it is already here! From the moment we ask God to be part of our lives, His kingdom is established inside us. His love, His compassion, His mercy, and His grace begin to change us from the inside out.

But to live solidly in the kingdom of God, we must fully abandon ourselves to God's mercy and love and totally place our hope in Him. We must rest by His feet daily in prayer and meditate on His Word. We must be earnest and wholehearted believers in Him—His loyal subjects. And that is when His kingdom reigns!

∽◎◎◠

Precious Father, my secret pal and I are eager to know the righteousness, peace, and joy that come from Your kingdom. We surrender ourselves to Your kingship and thank You for Your indwelling presence in our lives. Amen.

Patience

**I waited patiently for the LORD;
and he inclined unto me,
and heard my cry.**

PSALM 40:1 KJV

Dear Secret Pal,

*C*an you think of anything more difficult than waiting? I know I struggle with it, especially in the midst of a hectic lifestyle. How quickly my patience wears threadbare when someone or something doesn't move according to my expectations. But one thing I have learned; God is worth waiting for.

When I feel myself growing frustrated over answers that don't come and expectations that remain unfulfilled, I pour out my heart to God and lay my troubles at His feet. It's true that He may not solve them instantly—that's what patience is all about. But He will listen and comfort me if only I will let Him. Wait for Him, dear friend. You will not be disappointed.

*K*ind Father, help my secret pal as she strives to wait on You and lay her troubles at Your feet. Fill her with confident hope and quiet expectation. Amen.

Believing and Receiving God's Promises

**As for God, his way is perfect.
All the LORD's promises prove true.
He is a shield for all who look to him for protection.**

2 SAMUEL 22:31 NLT

Dear Secret Pal,

*B*elieving God's promises is receiving God's promises. It all begins with faith. Through faith we meet God halfway, reaching out for His hand. In effect, we say, "I have heard Your promises, O Lord, and I accept! Thank You for this unearned bounty and goodness! I am unspeakably blessed to be Your child! Praise You, God of all creation!"

When we accept and embrace God's incredible promises, we abound in love, peace, and joy. His way is perfect. We become like beacons of hope to those who long for more. Open your heart, dear friend, to believe and receive God's goodness.

*G*od, my Father, I am overwhelmed and forever changed by Your infinite goodness to me. Continue to bless my secret pal and me as we embrace Your promises in every area of our lives! Amen.

Faith, Hope, Love

**And now abide faith, hope, love, these three;
but the greatest of these is love.**

1 CORINTHIANS 13:13 NKJV

Dear Secret Pal,

*O*h, what a beautiful thing it would be to constantly live in faith, hope, and love, and to believe in God with a pure, childlike faith—the kind that moves mountains, changes hearts, plants seeds, and affects everything we touch. Or to nurture a bright and positive hope in all things, believing the best of others, seeing the light at the end of the tunnel, having the confidence that the present and future burst with promise. To be filled with faith and hope—wouldn't it be great!

But the greatest, by far, of these three—faith, hope, love—is love. Jesus, more than anything else, taught about love. And He demonstrated true and perfect love by giving His life for us. What wonderful blessings we receive from Him, dear friend. Let's open our hearts to receive until we are full to overflowing.

---

*L*ord God, teach my secret pal and me to embrace faith and hope—but even more, let us hold fast to love. And let us offer our hearts to the Author of love and learn from Him. Amen.

Discipline

**O Lord, your discipline is good
and leads to life and health.
Oh, heal me and make me live!**

ISAIAH 38:16 TLB

Dear Secret Pal,

I used to think of discipline in a negative sense. But spiritual discipline is training and exercise that helps us build spiritual muscles, strengthening us to live our lives to the fullest.

We become more spiritually disciplined as we enjoy a regular prayer life, allowing God to make us reflections of His true image. He may lead us to other forms of discipline, like memorizing Scripture, volunteering to help others, or joining a Bible study group. All these things will strengthen us and solidify our relationship with Him. So let's agree together to pursue discipline as a positive way to please God and help us attain a happy, fulfilled life.

---

*W*ise Father, as my secret pal and I bow our heads together, we ask that You grant us the grace necessary to apply Your discipline to our lives. Amen.

God's Word, Our Strength

**For the word of God is living and powerful,
and sharper than any two-edged sword.**

HEBREWS 4:12 NKJV

Dear Secret Pal,

*N*ever underestimate the power of God's Word. Even the most learned Bible scholar will admit that there are many things he or she does not understand. That's because the Bible is a spiritual book, filled with mysteries that we can understand only as God reveals them to us. God's Word will never come alive when we read only with our minds, tuning out our hearts.

If you ask God to help you, He will place His words in Your heart, almost as if He were whispering words of love and encouragement right into your ear. And when you listen and respond, you will be strengthened. As you read today, ask God to open your eyes to see the truth He has hidden in plain sight.

---

*G*entle Father, please help us hear and experience Your living Word with our spiritual ears—and change our hearts and our minds to think more like You. Amen.

Faithfulness of God

**He passed in front of Moses and said, "I am the LORD,
I am the LORD, the merciful and gracious God.
I am slow to anger and rich in unfailing love
and faithfulness."**

EXODUS 34:6 NLT

Dear Secret Pal,

God's faithfulness is such a force in our lives that we can see it and feel it. If you look with your heart, you will see His hand in every detail of your life. Certain things happen or don't happen because of Him. He creates opportunities, discoveries, and successes to encourage our hearts. And every good thing that comes our way issues from Him. He is always there for us.

God's faithfulness reassures us and gives us the comfort that flows from His unwavering and steadfast love. He is our God, and we are His children. He will never, ever abandon us. When we call upon Him, He will answer!

God of all creation, thank You for the immeasurable blessing of Your steadfast love! My secret pal and I desire to walk in it more fully every day. Amen.

The Church

We took sweet counsel together,
And walked to the house of God in the throng.

PSALM 55:14 NKJV

Dear Secret Pal,

*H*ave you ever wondered why churches are so different? In one country, a congregation gathers beneath a palm-thatched roof, their bare feet tapping the rhythm on a packed-dirt floor as they jubilantly sing hymns and praise songs. In another country, people gather in an ancient stone cathedral where magnificent stained-glass windows cast jewel-toned patterns across a marble floor. But these qualities do not make up a church. Instead, a real church is determined by the hearts of the believers who fellowship there.

Nothing bolsters our spirits quite like gathering with other believers to worship and praise our almighty, living God. Whether we wear designer suits or old tattered jeans, it is the assembling together that gives us the opportunity we need to unite our hearts and rise above the "humanness" of our lives. I hope you have found a church family with whom to worship.

---

*L*ord God, coming together with Your people is a great blessing here on earth. Thank You for reminding us that we are part of a family. Amen.

Obedience

**From my earliest youth I have tried to obey you;
your Word has been my comfort.**

PSALM 119:52 TLB

Dear Secret Pal,

*I*f we love God, we will obey Him. Like any good father, He has given us simple precepts by which to live. His intention is not to inhibit us but to free us to live life to the fullest. Like the rules of driving, they keep us out of accidents and on the road to our destination.

It could be that you have never thought of God's commandments as a road map to an abundant and happy life. But that's exactly what they are. They allow us to live together in peace, love, and harmony. And all of the commandments can be summed up in one—love. If we obey that command, the rest will follow naturally. So you see, dear friend, by being obedient, we wrap ourselves in God's love.

*R*ighteous Father, thank You for the kindness You show to us through Your commandments. Help us always remember that they are principles for a happy and fulfilled life. Amen.

Endurance

For you have need of endurance,
so that after you have done the will of God,
you may receive the promise.

HEBREWS 10:36 NKJV

Dear Secret Pal,

God has His own idea of timing. You have probably learned, as I have, that He does not often answer in the way we expect. In other words, we find many opportunities to wait for God's answer, and that requires endurance.

Hanging on to God and waiting for what He has promised helps us develop endurance, and endurance makes us strong, patient children, willing to wait for God's very best answer. Put your trust in Him, dear friend. He will come to your aid. He will show you the way. He will give you the answer you seek. And you will be stronger because you waited and trusted in Him.

Sweet Lord, we place our trust in You. We wait for You with the patient confidence that comes from waiting on Your best for every situation of our lives. Amen.

Strength

**The LORD is my strength,
the reason for my song,
because he has saved me.**

EXODUS 15:2 CEV

∽⊚⊚∾

Dear Secret Pal,

As you become accustomed to facing life's challenges with God at your side, your heart will become confident and secure, able to accomplish great things. You will become less vulnerable to the fear and anxiety that can rob you of your strength and vigor.

Place your faith in Him, dear friend. Wholly embrace His love and His watchful care over you. I have. And I have found strength and courage that I never knew I had. In fact, they are not products of my own resolve at all, but the result of God's faithful hand lifting and carrying me. Turn your burdens over to Him. His strength will uphold you, and His love will keep you.

∽⊚⊚∾

All-powerful and loving God, although it seems inconceivable that You would care for us as You do, we wholly embrace Your precious love and accept the invincible strength that is ours as Your children. Amen.

Praise Him

O Lord, I will honor and praise your name,
for you are my God.
You do such wonderful things!

Isaiah 25:1 nlt

Dear Secret Pal,

*K*nowing God is the most exciting thing I've ever experienced. As I become more aware of His love and goodness, my heart longs to clap, shout, and dance for joy! My voice wants to burst forth in song and make beautiful music for the whole world to hear! My whole being aches to celebrate His loyalty and compassion, to shout for joy that He has redeemed me!

We were created to praise Him. When we praise God with honest and open hearts, we discover a deep spiritual connection that links our spirits to His and at the same time fills us with love and compassion for the world around us. Close your eyes and focus on His goodness. And then release your soul to Him and let it take flight!

*L*ord God, You deserve all our love and thanksgiving! We give it to You now. We lift up our voices in song to You. We open our hearts to praise Your name. Amen.

The Holy Spirit

**You should know that your body is a temple
for the Holy Spirit who is in you.
You have received the Holy Spirit from God.
So you do not belong to yourselves.**

1 CORINTHIANS 6:19 NCV

Dear Secret Pal,

God sends His Holy Spirit to inspire, guide, and protect us. He fully understands that we need help to live victorious lives, and He gives His Holy Spirit to become our personal Helper to lead and teach us throughout our day and to be our Spirit of truth. The Holy Spirit works through God's people to show the world the truth about God.

God manifests great power in us through the Holy Spirit—power for success, power for victory, power to carry out His will for our lives. But in order to fully avail ourselves of this immense source of spiritual strength, we must cultivate our relationship with both the Father and His Spirit, training our spiritual ears to hear and respond to His "still, small voice."

Sweet Holy Spirit, we are honored to give You room in our hearts. Use us for Your important work today and every day. Amen.

A Lamp to Our Feet

Your word is a lamp to my feet
And a light to my path.

PSALM 119:105 NKJV

Dear Secret Pal,

Have you ever walked down a trail on a dark, moonless night without a flashlight? It doesn't take long to realize it's hopeless, not to mention dangerous. That's how it is when we try to navigate our way through life without the guiding light of God's Word. God's Word not only brings warmth and light and comfort, but it enlightens us by showing us how to proceed without stumbling over every obstacle along the way.

So why would we go anywhere without God's Word to light our way? We must fill our hearts and our minds with Scripture. By reading, meditating, memorizing, even singing God's words, we incorporate His light inside of us—we become living lamps, shining God's true, pure light to all around us.

Lord God, please light our way with the precious light of Your living Word. And fill our hearts and our minds so that we may shine forth Your glory! Amen.

Serving God

**Your faith makes you offer your lives
as a sacrifice in serving God. . . .
You also should be happy
and full of joy with me.**

PHILIPPIANS 2:17-18 NCV

Dear Secret Pal,

As our faith grows and develops, we long to wholeheartedly serve the Lord. We begin to see the shallowness of our human endeavors—material possessions, pleasures of the flesh, social status—things that mean nothing to our relationship with God.

And it's at this point of our faith journey that we reach the threshold of achieving the greatest satisfaction that we as God's children can know in this life: the joy of serving our Lord with our whole being. If you have known God in this way, dear friend, then you know as well as I that it is more wonderful than our hearts could imagine. If you have not experienced the fullness of serving God, then I urge you to do so. You will never be sorry.

Dear God, strengthen our purpose and direction so we may serve You with our whole hearts. Amen.

Temptations

**God can be trusted not to allow you to suffer any temptation
beyond your powers of endurance.
He will see to it that every temptation has its way out,
so that it will be possible for you to bear it.**

1 CORINTHIANS 10:13 PHILLIPS

Dear Secret Pal,

Temptation comes into our lives in many different ways. It may be in the enticing form of a thick slice of fudge. Or in the lure to spend money on something we know we can't afford. Or perhaps on something even more serious. Whatever it is, temptation comes. It's as inescapable as the air we breathe, and it's all part of the human condition. But no assault of temptation is unique—we all experience it from time to time.

Yet God promises that if we trust Him, He will help us endure and ultimately escape in one piece. Though temptation is difficult to resist sometimes, it is always worth it! For our Father truly knows what's best. And because He loves us, He wants the best for us!

Father God, we ask for Your help and guidance in times of temptation. Teach us to turn quickly to You and to trust You so that we may escape into Your arms of love. Amen.

Stewardship

**Work hard and cheerfully at whatever you do,
as though you were working for the Lord rather than for
people. Remember that the Lord will give you
an inheritance as your reward.**

COLOSSIANS 3:23-24 NLT

Dear Secret Pal,

Stewardship is all about making the best use of what God has given us. And once we realize that God has given us all we have, we will begin to see our material blessings as God's vehicles to love and transform the world. When we accept that all our wealth and gifts and blessings come directly from God's hand, we begin to understand how these things are abundant and renewable and eternal.

We begin to appreciate how our talents and aptitudes aren't merely for our own delight and personal prosperity. They are on loan to us from God. All of us—whether a talented businessperson, artist, teacher, technician, or factory worker—all have important gifts to use to glorify His Name!

O Lord, help us to remember that we belong to You and are accountable to You for how we use the gifts You have given us. Amen.

Answered Prayer

**It shall come to pass
That before they call, I will answer;
And while they are still speaking,
I will hear.**

ISAIAH 65:24 NKJV

Dear Secret Pal,

*J*ust as an earthly father enjoys presenting a new gift to his kids, so our Heavenly Father delights in giving us good gifts. He loves to hear our prayers, and He loves to answer us. Of course, sometimes His answers are "no" or "wait," but we must realize He alone knows what's truly best for us.

As we grow spiritually in our relationship with Him, we become more attuned to His ways, and subsequently we pray more in accordance with His will and purpose for our lives. That is when God can truly give us the desires of our hearts. Pray with confidence today, dear friend. God hears you.

---

*D*ear Father God, teach us how to pray in partnership with You, trusting in Your divine purpose for our lives. Amen.

Forgiveness

*Your heavenly Father will forgive you
if you forgive those who sin against you;
but if you refuse to forgive them, he will not forgive you.*

MATTHEW 6:14 TLB

Dear Secret Pal,

*L*ove fosters forgiveness. If we obey the command to love God and our neighbor, the "forgiveness seed" is already planted in our hearts. Perhaps we've heard this statement so much that its revolutionary message becomes lost to us. But just think how it would impact the world if people everywhere consistently forgave each other when they were wronged! War would cease. Hatred, enmity, violence, crime, and sin would be no more. People would not feud or harbor grudges. Anger would dissolve.

A universal spirit of love and forgiveness could transform this world! And if peace ruled, imagine all the time, energy, and resources that could be redistributed in fruitful ways; humanity's works would become a fountain of praise to God!

*D*ear Father, give us continual grace to spur forgiveness in our hearts; we know and understand that You will forgive us according to the quality of forgiveness we have shown others. Amen.

Happiness

Happy is the man who finds wisdom,
And the man who gains understanding;
For her proceeds are better than the profits of silver,
And her gain than fine gold.

PROVERBS 3:13 NKJV

Dear Secret Pal,

If you asked the average person on the street what it would take to make his or her life happier, many would say "more money." Yet when I look at some of the world's richest and most famous people, they don't appear to be truly happy. What they don't realize is true happiness can be found only in God.

When we give our lives over to Him, the wellspring of all things good, He begins to fill us with His wisdom and understanding. And in that wisdom and understanding, the seed of true happiness dwells. We were created to have fellowship with our Creator—this is the only true source of happiness.

O Most High, teach us to seek Your wisdom and to fill our hearts with Your understanding. For only then will we know true happiness, happiness that is founded in You. Amen.

Responsibility

**Verily I say unto you, Inasmuch as ye have done it
unto one of the least of these my brethren,
ye have done it unto me.**

MATTHEW 25:40 KJV

Dear Secret Pal,

For the believer, such excuses as "It's not my job" or "It doesn't concern me" have no application when it comes to helping others. Faith without works doesn't exist. If we accept God's love and embrace His commands, we cannot turn away from others' needs. For if we ignore our hurting and hungry fellowman, it is as if we have turned our back on God. When we offer a kind and helping hand to those in need, we delight the heart of God.

Our love for God compels us to reach out; it motivates us to help others with strength that is not our own. And then this love overflows to the rest of His creation. And this is His beautiful plan—that we might be His hands, that we might reach out in love and comfort to help a hurting world.

Dear Father, grant us the energy and stamina to be Your constant light to the world. Help us fully use all You have given us for the sake of others. Amen.

God's Will for Our Lives

**Be happy in your faith at all times.
Never stop praying.
Be thankful, whatever the circumstances may be.
For this is the will of God for you in Christ Jesus.**

1 THESSALONIANS 5:16-18 PHILLIPS

Dear Secret Pal,

I've noticed that many people wander through life wondering what they should be doing. They are good people, but they don't seem to have much direction. For some, that might be because they're looking for answers in the wrong places. Others want to know all the answers before they can go forward.

Through prayer and meditation, Bible study and interaction with other believers, we can understand His will as it pertains to us. Although God's whole plan for us may not be clearly outlined, if we trust in His love and read His Word, He will show us where to go step by step, day by day. And it is only as we abide in His will that we find joyful satisfaction.

Lord God, thank You for creating a special plan for each and every life. Guide my secret pal and me as we endeavor to walk in the path You have set for our feet. Amen.

Stability

**The Lord is my helper, and I will not
fear what man shall do unto me. . . .
Jesus Christ the same yesterday,
and to day, and for ever.**

HEBREWS 13:6,8 KJV

⌘⌘⌘

Dear Secret Pal,

Life can sometimes make us feel as if we are walking on eggshells—
very unstable. People say one thing, then do another. Values and morals shift
and change like the tide. Yet how we hunger for stability and security. People
are constantly searching for something solid enough to cling to, something
they can trust in, someone they can rely upon. Nothing seems to stay the
same—except God.

God is the Rock upon whom we can stand. He is the Anchor that keeps
us from drifting out to sea. He is the stabilizing force within our shaky
little worlds. He is acutely aware that the things of this world are rapidly
changing—He's been watching it since the beginning of time. There are no
surprises for God. You can safely place Your trust in Him.

⌘⌘⌘

Precious Lord, my secret pal and I have decided to put our trust
in You, for You are unshakeable and unchangeable. Amen.

Doubt

**Behold, the LORD's hand is not shortened,
that it cannot save;
neither his ear heavy,
that it cannot hear.**

ISAIAH 59:1 KJV

Dear Secret Pal,

Sometimes it seems as if doubts are as unpredictable as the weather. We go through sweet times when we feel strong and confident, and then, wham, like a gray, gloomy cloud full of rain, doubt pelts us with cold, wet uncertainty. The important thing to remember, my friend, is that the storm will taper off, and God will remain, shining His radiant warmth like golden sunlight all over our lives.

And like the weather, perhaps there is no real way to prevent some doubts from falling like raindrops upon us. Perhaps the question is how we react to them when they hit. We must remember that God is bigger, stronger, and greater than the doubts that assault us.

Heavenly Father, help my secret pal and me to focus our eyes on Your greatness and watch our doubts vanish in the light of Your glory. Amen.

Counting Our Blessings

**O give thanks unto the LORD;
for he is good:
for his mercy endureth for ever.**

PSALM 136:1 KJV

◦◉◦

Dear Secret Pal,

Every good thing comes from the Lord. Whatever blessings we have, including the miraculous gift of life itself, issue from God's infinite love. I like to take a moment every day to look around and number the many good things God has given me. In so doing, I try not to limit my search to earthly things, but instead look into my heart and mind—for they are the repositories of God's richest blessings.

This simple exercise is especially helpful when I feel low or "blue." Without fail, it restores a proper perspective in my life. Through God, it is possible to have everything I need to give my life meaning and purpose. Let's open our hearts and praise Him for all He has given us.

————————— ◦◉◦ —————————

Heavenly Father, our Source of happiness and security, we praise You and thank You for the innumerable good things You have given us. We are truly blessed to be Your children. Amen.

Growing in the Spirit

*You must make every effort
to support your faith with goodness,
and goodness with knowledge,
and knowledge with self-control,
and self-control with endurance,
and endurance with godliness.*

2 PETER 1:5-6 NRSV

Dear Secret Pal,

The wonderful thing about faith is that once established in our hearts, it will grow ever larger, stronger, and more delightful. Like a tree, our spiritual lives can reach great heights if our roots are grounded in Him.

And like a tree, our reach becomes wider, broader, and more encompassing until we are able to offer the world more and more of God's living love. God wants us to be strong and sturdy, rooted in Him and able to withstand the storms and the wind. Let God establish His truth in your heart.

Almighty and merciful Lord, Your gift of living faith and the means You give us to nourish it are beyond our comprehension, yet they are the wellspring of our joy! Thank you. Amen.

Humility

**The reward for humility and fear of the LORD
is riches and honor and life.**

PROVERBS 22:4 NRSV

Dear Secret Pal,

Humility is sometimes confused with low self-esteem. But true and pure humility is the direct result of understanding and revering the greatness, majesty, and might of God. When we bow at His feet, fully aware of His power and glory, we are humbled. We see how small and insignificant we are compared to His holy splendor. We see ourselves with true humility. And yet, as magnificent and powerful as God is, He reaches out His hand of kindness and lifts us up!

How amazing that the mighty King of all kings, deeming us worthy of His affection, should reach out with such compassion toward us. But we know His thrilling and generous gift of grace is undeserved. And in sweet humility we cling to Him, praising and thanking Him for loving us so completely.

Dear Lord, we humbly acknowledge all that You have done for us. We thank You and praise Your name. Amen.

God the Father

Have we not all one Father?
Has not one God created us?

MALACHI 2:10 MLB

Dear Secret Pal,

*E*ven the best earthly father cannot meet all of his children's varying and changing needs. It's just not humanly possible. For God has designed our hearts from the beginning of time to long for a depth of nurturing and love and acceptance that only He can provide. Nothing else satisfies. And because He loves us, God desires to father us completely. He longs to teach and instruct our minds, to comfort and care for our hurts, to shape our spirits and transform our hearts.

But like shy children, we sometimes hold back—afraid to let go and run freely into our Father's arms. But He is always there, waiting with arms open wide, ever ready to forgive us and love us and lead us into His glorious kingdom.

*H*eavenly Father, my secret pal and I come to You now like children full of expectation. Receive us as we rush into Your loving arms. Amen.

Justice

**By me kings reign, and rulers decree
what is just; by me rulers rule,
and nobles, all who govern rightly.**

PROVERBS 8:15-16 NRSV

Dear Secret Pal,

*T*rue and lasting justice can be found only in God. He is a merciful judge, full of grace and loving-kindness. For if He judged us by our own words and deeds, we would surely fall short and be sentenced to condemnation. But because He allowed His own Son to be sentenced to death for our sins, we have obtained glorious access into His presence and kingdom.

And what can we learn about justice from God? When we are wronged or mistreated by those around us, instead of demanding retribution or exacting revenge, we can raise ourselves up to the level of our Savior and forgive. It's a strange form of justice that the world cannot comprehend. It is a reflection of God's pure and unconditional love.

*M*ighty God, teach us to understand Your justice. Show us when and how we can show mercy and loving-kindness to those who wrongfully hurt us. Amen.

Protection

**Fear not, for I am with you; be not dismayed,
for I am your God! I will strengthen you,
yes, I will help you; yes, I will uphold you
with My vindicating right hand.**

ISAIAH 41:10 MLB

Dear Secret Pal,

*D*o you find yourself longing for protection as I do? I think we all want the security of a solid roof over our heads, a good insurance policy, and a well-trained, responsive police force. Yet even with those earthly protections in place, we are still vulnerable to the unexpected perils of life. That's why we need the assurance that God is with us, that He is at hand and standing guard. Then we can relax and rest in His safekeeping.

Remember, dear friend, God's protection reaches much deeper than the mere physical realm. He desires to guard and defend our hearts as well. Spiritual forces will wage war against us, but when we trust in God, relying on His strength for our defense, we will arise victoriously!

*D*ear Father, we offer our praise and thanksgiving to You, for You are our great Protector! You alone have won the victory! Thank You! Amen.

God's Provision

**My God will fully satisfy every need of yours
according to his riches in glory in Christ Jesus.
To our God and Father be glory
forever and ever. Amen.**

PHILIPPIANS 4:19-20 NRSV

Dear Secret Pal,

What do we really need to live? Food? Water? Clothing? God has provided us with all those things, and yet sometimes we still feel so very needy. Perhaps we confuse need with want.

When we come before God each day, asking Him to show us what our needs truly are, and trusting in His provision, our perspective changes. We begin to see that our spiritual needs are deeper than our physical ones. And we begin to understand that God's riches in glory consist of eternal, priceless things, like love, joy, and peace. God longs to provide for us, more than we can even ask or imagine!

Dear Lord, my secret pal and I bow before You and ask You to show us what we truly need. Fill our hearts with praise for all You have provided. Amen.

Garden of Friends

**Beloved, let us love one another,
because love springs from God.**

1 JOHN 4:7 MLB

Dear Secret Pal,

God has not created us to dwell in isolation. He has placed others in and around our lives, creatively connecting us to special people to whom we can relate, who understand our hearts and encourage our spirits. We call these people friends.

But like a lovely garden of flowers, friendships need time and care and nurturing. When neglected, they may become weedy or wilted and may eventually die. We need to generously water these friendships with our love, nourish them with rich doses of grace, and occasionally pull out a few weeds of resentment. These tasks will cause us to reap lovely relationships that enhance many areas of our lives with their fragrance and their beauty. And God is pleased.

Dear Lord, show us how to better tend our garden of friends, to take care with each individual, and to rejoice in the benefits of healthy friendships. Amen.

In His Image

Be therefore imitators of God
as His beloved children, and live in love,
as Christ also loved us and gave Himself for us,
an offering and sacrifice to God.

EPHESIANS 5:1-2 MLB

Dear Secret Pal,

I used to play dress-up when I was a small child. How about you?
I think it's natural for children to want to dress up in their parents' clothes
and pretend to be "just like Mommy" or "just like Daddy."

If we are truly God's children, it will be natural for us to imitate Him
as well. We can slip our little selves into Christlike qualities of
unconditional love for those around us or try on a perfect set of patience or
wear a covering of lovely peace that passes all understanding. Will others
look at us and see that we look a little bit like our Father? Without a doubt,
imitating God is an important step in our spiritual development.

Heavenly Father, make us imitators of You, adorning ourselves in
the beautiful qualities that show the world we are truly Your children.
Amen.

In Our Weakness

**I have learned both to be full and to be hungry,
both to abound and to suffer need.
I can do all things through Christ
who strengthens me.**

PHILIPPIANS 4:12-13 NKJV

❧

Dear Secret Pal,

*A*re you one of those people who always strive to keep the body strong? I am, too. I try to eat right and take my vitamins. I've started many new exercise programs through the years, all in hopes of becoming stronger, fitter, and healthier. Who in their right mind would knowingly strive toward weakness?

And yet we are all weak in some areas. But God says that's okay. When we learn to recognize and accept our areas of weakness, we can then hand them over to Him. That's where the miracle begins. In that moment of confession, He makes us strong in Him, because it's only in our weakness that God is able to bestow His power upon us. That's when God is truly glorified.

❧

O mighty God, we know our areas of weakness. Pour out Your grace on us as we hand them over to You. Amen.

Peace

**Those of steadfast mind you keep in peace—
in peace because they trust in you.**

ISAIAH 26:3 NRSV

Dear Secret Pal,

We all long for a peaceful escape from the noise and chaos of our hectic lives—the ring of the telephone, the bustle of a busy household, the demands of a job, even the responsibilities of raising children often weigh heavily upon us. We might even imagine a private refuge somewhere—perhaps a cabin tucked deep in the trees, where all is quiet. However, such escapes are few and far between.

But God's peace can be found in the midst of these turbulent times—when we need it most! But we must focus our hearts on Him and remember how tenderly He loves and cares for us. This ignites our trust and allows us to rest securely. Then, and only then, can we find real and lasting peace.

O God of peace and comfort, we come to You now with trusting hearts and ask You to fill us, once again, with Your perfect peace that passes all understanding. Amen.

God, Our Savior

**My heart is overflowing with praise of my Lord,
my soul is full of joy in God my Saviour.
For he has deigned to notice me, his humble servant, and all
generations to come will call me the happiest of women!**

LUKE 1:46-48 PHILLIPS

Dear Secret Pal,

Have you ever imagined being rescued by an armor-clad knight mounted upon his sturdy steed? Of course, that is the stuff of which fairy tales are made, but it's not so very different from the reality of what we have in God. For He is Rescuer, dear Friend, powerful Redeemer! And He has overcome every obstacle in order to gather us unto Himself.

Almighty God, from the beginning of time, chose to display His love for us in a most extraordinary way, coming to our rescue with might and power. But as mighty as He is, God cannot redeem us unless we allow Him to do so. Let's agree to reach out our hands and grasp His, today and every day of our lives.

Almighty God, we come to You now in thanksgiving that You are our Savior. And once again we reach out to You and grasp Your strong hand of salvation. We cling to it. Amen.

The Divine Difference

**Whoever does not love does not know God,
for God is love.**

1 JOHN 4:8 NRSV

Dear Secret Pal,

*L*ove. They talk of it on television and in movies, magazines, and books. And yet without God, there exists no real, true, selfless love. Sure, there may be brotherly affection, friendly devotion, physical desire, and even lust. But perfect love is found only in our loving and living God.

And He longs for us to love one another the way He first loved us. He longs for us to give selflessly, to forgive easily, to show endless mercy, and to encourage one another. But first we must surrender our hearts and minds in a conscious choice to know and to love Him. Then He will miraculously impart the grace required to love others in this amazing way. God's love in us is a sharp contrast to the world's version of love. But that, dear friend, is the divine difference!

*D*ear Father, all glory is Yours for loving us with an everlasting love. Pour Your love through us so we might love others as You do, and the world might know the difference! Amen.

Holiness

*But from Him you have your existence in Christ Jesus,
who became for us divine wisdom and righteousness
and holiness and redemption.*

1 CORINTHIANS 1:30 MLB

৶⊚৶

Dear Secret Pal,

*How can our human minds ever fully understand the vast and
expansive meaning of true holiness? We know that God is holy, but how do
we comprehend this concept while living in this physical world?*

*Perhaps we can get a tiny glimpse of holiness as we stand before the
awesome power of the ocean pounding against the shoreline rocks. Or maybe
we can see it in a glorious sunset that dramatically paints the sky with
vibrant shades of coral, magenta, and purple. Or it may be seen even in the
quiet, miracle of birth when a sweet newborn utters its first cry. All these
wonders prime our spirits for that day when we gather before Him singing,
"Holy, holy, holy!"*

───────────── ৶⊚৶ ─────────────

*O Holy God, Your holiness is too magnificent for us to grasp. But
please give us glimpses along the path of our earthly lives so our hearts
might prepare for that day when we see Your holiness face to face.
Amen.*

Sacrifice

**Whoever wishes to be great among you
must be your servant.**

MATTHEW 20:26 NRSV

Dear Secret Pal,

*S*acrifices were common in Jesus' time. They were the way most cultures chose to show devotion and ask for restoration and blessings from their gods. Unlike the pagan gods served by so many, the one true God provided His own sacrifice, perfect and worthy. When Jesus, God's only begotten Son, laid down His life for all, no other sacrifice was ever needed. He became the final sacrifice, and the atonement was complete. "It is finished," He cried from the cross.

We are no longer required to make sacrifices to God, except as we imitate His sacrificial love for us in our dealings with others. Those who have done this testify that they have received much more than they have given—treasures like peace, joy, and happiness. For the truth is, we cannot outgive God!

---

*D*ear loving and generous Father, please reveal to us ways that we can lay down our lives as a living sacrifice to You, that we might show You how much we love You. Amen.

Exalting God's Name

**Magnify the LORD with me
and let us exalt His name together.**

PSALM 34:3 MLB

Dear Secret Pal,

Have you ever noticed how many names there are for God? Lord of lords, Deliverer, King of kings, Almighty God, Savior, Heavenly Father, the Good Shepherd, and the Holy One—just to name a few. If you look into the Hebrew you will discover dozens more. All these names are appropriate, for how can you describe God using only one word?

And when we come before Him, it's fitting to call Him by His many wonderful names. Each name is significant for how we relate to Him at any given moment. We call Him Majesty when awestruck by His power. We call Him Father when we long to be gathered into His arms. We call Him Savior when we need to be rescued. The names for God are as limitless as His being. And we can creatively assign names to Him that only we will know.

---

*O sweet **Papa God**, hold me in Your strong and loving arms. I worship You by all Your names. I praise every facet of Your mighty being. Amen.*

Redemption

**So overflowing is his kindness towards us that he took away
all our sins through the blood of his Son,
by whom we are saved;
and he has showered down upon us the richness of his grace.**

EPHESIANS 1:7 TLB

Dear Secret Pal,

*R*edemption suggests the act of saving something that for one reason or another has become lost or worthless. And that accurately describes what happens in our lives when God touches them. How amazing that God gazes down upon us, when, indeed, others might just shake their heads and walk by. God pauses long enough to really see us. His eyes are full of mercy as He, in His wisdom, recognizes something of innate value in us. And He, the mighty God, the Creator of the universe, stoops to pick us up.

In that unforgettable moment, our blessed Redeemer has saved us by grace. Then we, dear friend, are redeemed! We are sealed by grace, to belong forevermore to the great Redeemer.

*D*ear blessed Redeemer, all praise and thanksgiving are Yours! Thank You for reaching down to save us when no one else believed we were worthy. Amen.

Overcoming

**Do not, therefore, abandon that confidence of yours;
it brings a great reward. For you need endurance,
so that when you have done the will of God,
you may receive what was promised.**

HEBREWS 10:35-36 NRSV

Dear Secret Pal,

*N*o one ever said following God would be easy. However, when faced with new challenges, we often forget where we've been and where we're going. When we can no longer see the reward ahead, we easily become overwhelmed.

Good marathon runners keep the finish line in mind throughout the long race, pacing themselves carefully, running neither too fast nor too slow, considering the energy needed to reach the end. The same principle applies as we move forward in our lives toward God. We must pace ourselves daily, confidently stride forward, and realize that we will eventually overcome life's challenges and finish our race victoriously!

*D*ear Lord, make us overcomers as we daily pace ourselves in our race toward Your kingdom, confident that You are running right alongside, encouraging us all the way. Amen.

Getting Personal with God

**Look! I have been standing at the door
and I am constantly knocking.
If anyone hears me calling him and opens the door,
I will come in and fellowship with him and he with me.**

REVELATION 3:20 TLB

Dear Secret Pal,

All human beings long for intimacy; don't you agree? We were created with a deep need for understanding, empathy, compassion, and love in order to draw us to our Maker. He longs to know us intimately, to share our secrets, to listen to our dreams, to heal our hurts.

Indeed He stands at the door of our hearts, knocking persistently. And all we must do is say, "Come in, Lord." He will enter and immediately sit down and share intimate and wonderful fellowship with us. How many times have we sat alone, longing for someone to meet us in this manner? And He was present all the time, waiting for us to invite Him in.

Lord God, my secret pal and I long to have fellowship with You and know You better. It is good to know that You are always with us. Amen.

Purpose of Life

**Call to me and I will answer you,
and will tell you great and hidden things
that you have not known.**

JEREMIAH 33:3 NRSV

Dear Secret Pal,

*H*ave you noticed how easily we become caught up in the daily treadmill of life? We get stuck juggling responsibilities, commuting back and forth, and caring for others. Soon we begin to think that that's all there is. We forget the true purpose in life—or perhaps we have never completely figured it out.

However, God makes it clear that our highest purpose in life is to love. Now that may seem simple enough, but it isn't always easy. We know we must love God, others, and ourselves, and He provides numerous hands-on opportunities to practice that love each day. Yet if we become caught up in the treadmill, we miss these opportunities, and life becomes dull and mundane. When you feel that happening, simply say, "Oops, I've forgotten to love." It's the best way to put purpose back into your life.

*D*ear loving God, remind us again of Your purposes for our lives. Show us how to love as You have loved us. Amen.

Truth

**Therefore, laying all falsehood aside,
speak truth each person to his neighbor,
for we are one another's members.**

EPHESIANS 4:25 MLB

Dear Secret Pal,

Nothing liberates our hearts quite like the truth. Honesty—like a fresh spring breeze, invigorating, cleansing, refreshing—truly does set us free! When we turn our backs on lies and hypocrisy, and instead choose to live in truth and honesty, we find that heavy burdens are lifted from our shoulders. We may even enjoy a better night's sleep. The benefits of truth are real and lasting. Why should we settle for anything less?

But we are not the only ones who benefit when we choose to embrace truth in our lives. The lives of those around us are also touched. For truth is a rare quality in the world today. When people see honesty at work in the lives of those who love God, they are encouraged to view God in a fresh new way, which brings hope and life.

O Most High, help us to have honest hearts and truthful tongues, that we might bring glory and honor and praise to You. Amen.

Wisdom

**The fear of the LORD is the beginning of wisdom,
and the knowledge of the Holy One is insight.**

PROVERBS 9:10 NRSV

ᐧᐧᐧ

Dear Secret Pal,

Even the most learned, most knowledgeable, and most highly educated person can lack wisdom. True wisdom comes only from God. It's a precious gift, more valuable than diamonds and worth seeking with our whole hearts. Yet in light of the world, wisdom is not easily found.

That's because the beginning of wisdom starts simply with knowing God. As we spend time in His presence, we learn more about Him. Fellowship with Him and meditation on His Word bring wisdom into our lives. Ironically, though, with the gaining of wisdom comes the knowledge of how very little we know. We realize that we could never be wise enough or gain too much wisdom. Yes, the pursuit of wisdom, like the pursuit of God, is an insatiable desire!

ᐧᐧᐧ

O Most Wise, help us to know You more, to understand Your ways, and to perceive Your truth. Then we will begin to experience Your wisdom. Amen.

Understanding

Don't let the world around you squeeze you into its own mould, but let God re-make you so that your whole attitude of mind is changed. Thus you will prove in practice that the will of God is good, acceptable to him and perfect.

ROMANS 12:2 PHILLIPS

Dear Secret Pal,

I don't know about you, but I have found that life becomes frustrating when I try to understand everything from my limited human perspective. I need more. I need to go to my Father in Heaven for help. For only God has all the answers. Only He can impart the kind of wisdom that enables me to deal with individuals and relationships with true understanding. But I must look to Him and ask.

And I must accept that at times He won't give me all the understanding I think I need. Sometimes the answers are too great for me to fully comprehend. God does promise to give me what I need for the day, and He will transform my mind to understand even more tomorrow. You can go to Him, too, my friend. He's always there to help.

Dear omniscient God, please teach us to turn to You for wisdom and understanding. Increase our trust and transform our minds. Amen.

Abundant Living

So the ransomed of the LORD shall return,
And come to Zion with singing,
With everlasting joy on their heads.
They shall obtain joy and gladness;
Sorrow and sighing shall flee away.

ISAIAH 51:11 NKJV

⁕

Dear Secret Pal,

Do you long, as I do, for the abundant life—to live each day fully, drinking in all the zest and happiness, giving and receiving with joy, celebrating each moment as a divine gift from God? And yet so much of the time we fall short by allowing ourselves to become overwhelmed by life's responsibilities. By the end of the day, we wonder if it was even worth our efforts. Yet God offers us so much more!

When we choose to praise God throughout our day, celebrating His goodness and mercy, we are changed—wonderfully and eternally changed! Our eyes begin to see the beauty around us, our hearts effuse with hope, and our efforts are blessed beyond imagination!

Heavenly Father, I desire to praise You throughout this day, looking to You to fulfill Your promise of abundant life. Amen.

A Servant's Heart

I will make the godly of the land my heroes,
and invite them to my home.
Only those who are truly good shall be my servants.

PSALM 101:6 TLB

Dear Secret Pal,

The life of a servant is not coveted by many. But the Son of the Most High left His glorious home in Heaven to come down to the darkness of earth to serve others. He fed the hungry, healed the sick, washed feet, and eventually laid down His life. He said we should also follow His example.

He taught us that true love means placing others above ourselves, thinking of their needs before our own. This isn't to say we should neglect ourselves (to do so would ultimately diminish our ability to love and to serve others), but rather God wants us to imitate Him by loving completely and thoroughly with hearts eager to serve. Miracles occur when we adopt a servant's heart: God is glorified, lives are touched, and we become like Him.

Dear Lord, teach us to adopt a servant's heart. Show us ways we can elevate others' needs above our own—that You might be glorified! Amen.

Worry

Don't worry about anything; instead, pray about everything; tell God your needs and don't forget to thank him for his answers.

಼ⓐⓖ಼

Dear Secret Pal,

Tiny seeds of worry can be planted in our lives, almost without our knowledge. When we hear troubling blurbs from media or friends, it can seem as if bad news floats through the air like fluffy dandelion seeds. Often we're unaware that these concerns have landed in our mind; but before we know it, they have grown, making us feel anxious.

God desires to keep us free from all anxiety. He wants to protect our hearts and minds with His peace and assurance. He wants us to give Him every little concern. By praying about everything and giving thanks, we allow God to remove those bothersome worry weeds, replacing them with His peace.

_____ ಼ⓐⓖ಼ _____

Precious Lord, my secret pal and I promise to take all our cares and worries to You. Thank You for loving us enough to remove the anxiety from our lives. Amen.

Caring for Others' Needs

Love one another as I have loved you.
No one has greater love than this,
to lay down one's life for one's friends.

JOHN 15:12-13 NRSV

Dear Secret Pal,

Merely saying the words "I love you" is easy enough, but actually acting on those words can present a big challenge. Rolling up our sleeves and showing others our love in active and practical ways can force us to step out of our comfort zone.

To offer this sort of help first requires compassion and commitment to care for those around us; then empathy to see when others are in need; finally, discernment to hear God's quiet voice as He gently leads and guides us. It isn't always easy to reach out to others. The sweet satisfaction that God plants in our hearts, however, is like nothing else on earth, and it's always rewarding.

O loving God, teach us Your compassion and write it on our hearts. Show us how to care for the needs of others, that we might glorify You! Amen.

Almighty Power of God

Begin to understand how incredibly great his power is to help those who believe him. It is that same mighty power that raised Christ from the dead and seated him in the place of honor at God's right hand in heaven.

EPHESIANS 1:19-20 TLB

Dear Secret Pal,

To fully understand the awesome, unfathomable power of Almighty God would most likely blow our little earth minds into millions of tiny pieces. No wonder so many scientists throw up their hands and deny God's deity altogether. The more we learn about this amazing world, the more we realize how powerful and great God is. That's where faith steps in.

By believing God, we allow Him to reveal Himself to us, a little bit each day. Even this limited knowledge fills us with wonder, for God is always far greater than our wildest imaginings. His power and mercy are perfect, unfailing, and eternal. We are not capable of understanding it, but we are able to praise Him for it!

O mighty God, Your ways are so much higher than ours. Help us understand Your power and glory just a little more. We offer You our humble praise. Amen.

Success

I have looked for You in the sanctuary,
To see Your power and Your glory.
Because Your lovingkindness is better than life,
My lips shall praise You.
Thus I will bless You while I live;
I will lift up my hands in Your name.

PSALM 63:2-4 NKJV

Dear Secret Pal,

How do you define success—wealth, celebrity, professional achievement, social status? Do you assume someone is doing well because he or she drives an expensive car?

God calls us to a higher level of success—a success of the heart, with our roots planted deeply in Him. He calls us to understand that His love and grace are far more valuable than life itself. He calls us to a place where our souls are at rest and richly satisfied. That, my friend, is the definition of true success and is worthy of our wholehearted pursuit.

O Lord, open our eyes to see how You define success. Teach our hearts to pursue Your forms of success with abandon. Amen.

Using Our Time Well

Christ . . . left behind an example, that you might follow in His footsteps.

1 PETER 2:21 MLB

cಲಿ⊚ฒ

Dear Secret Pal,

Time—the more we have, the more we waste. Isn't it true? When we think we have all the time in the world to do something, we usually put it off. But none of us knows how much time we really have. What if we put off doing something important today, like saying "I love you" to someone, and then tomorrow never comes? We must not forget that our days on earth are numbered. Only God knows that number.

Knowing that each day will never come again, we need to value our time, asking Him to guide us through every day. When we consider how Jesus' ministry lasted only three years yet changed the course of history forever, we might appreciate the number of our days in a whole new way.

———————— cಲಿ⊚ฒ ————————

Eternal Father, please teach us to respect the time that You've given us. Help us walk in Your counsel and use our days wisely, for Your glory and honor. Amen.

Emotional Healing

**He has sent me to bring good news to the oppressed,
to bind up the brokenhearted,
to proclaim liberty to the captives,
and release to the prisoners.**

ISAIAH 61:1 NRSV

Dear Secret Pal,

I always run to God when my heart is wounded and hurting. Do you? To whom do you run when circumstances leave you feeling lonely and confused? Can you trust His gentle hands to hold and heal you? Do you know that fixing broken hearts is His specialty and that He longs for you to go to Him even in the midst of your affliction?

No hurt is too small for God. Does a loving earthly father turn away his little child when she approaches him with a tiny sliver in her finger? No, he stoops down, gently removes the sliver, and then kisses her tiny fingertips. How much more will our Heavenly Father tenderly make you whole if you let Him!

*D*ear Great Physician, we believe You want to, and are able to, heal our hearts. Please help our unbelief. Teach us to come to You when we are hurting. Amen.

Joy

You love him even though you have never seen him.
Though you do not see him, you trust him; and even now
you are happy with a glorious, inexpressible joy.
Your reward for trusting him will be
the salvation of your souls.

1 PETER 1:8 9 NLT

Dear Secret Pal,

When was the last time you felt true joy? Can you remember? God longs for us to experience His joy on a regular basis.

Consider this: Have you ever physically seen God? Of course you've seen His creation and felt His touch on your life, but have you ever actually seen God with your very own eyes? Yet you love Him, don't you? How extraordinary! We love God with all our hearts, without ever having seen Him even once! That's simply because God, in all His glory, draws our hungry hearts to Him, and by grace compels our love. Doesn't that fill your heart with indescribably wonderful joy? And just think, that joy is merely a tiny taste of how wonderful Heaven will be!

Dear Lord, thank You for placing love in our hearts—love that brings us joy even when we have never even seen You. Amen.

Repentance

*You say, "We know that God's judgment on those
who do such things is in accordance with truth." . . .
Do you not realize that God's kindness
is meant to lead you to repentance?*

ROMANS 2:2,4 NRSV

∽⊙⊙∾

Dear Secret Pal,

*W*hat image comes to your mind when you hear the term "repent"?
Do you think of God's love and care for you?

True repentance is indeed a quiet and personal moment between us and
God. It is His kindness and gentleness that draw us to Him. He
encourages our hearts to seek out His loving touch. God waits patiently for
us, ever ready to forgive when we come before Him in deep sincerity and
heartfelt brokenness. He compassionately reaches out His hand of mercy as
we humbly bow before Him and confess our sins and express our regrets.
And with joy He listens as we thank Him for His grace and forgiveness.

―――――――――― ∽⊙⊙∾ ――――――――――

*D*ear forgiving Father, teach us to understand the loveliness of
repentance. Help us come before You with honest and sincere hearts, and
embrace with joy Your forgiveness. Amen.

God's Steadfast Love

**For God loved the world so much
that he gave his only Son
so that anyone who believes in him shall not perish
but have eternal life.**

JOHN 3:16 TLB

࿇

Dear Secret Pal,

God has loved us from the beginning of time. He loved us before we were born. And He loves us right now, right this very moment. God's love for us will last throughout eternity. It has never wavered but always has remained steadfast and true.

It's almost impossible to understand such steadfastness. Perhaps if we stand before a great ocean and watch the waves tumble in, never stopping, we might begin to understand; or if we look out into the starry night and consider how long those stars have been in place. Yet even these awesome parts of creation dim in comparison to God's steadfast love for us.

࿇

Loving Father, we cannot fathom Your steadfast love. It is too great and mighty for us to grasp. Yet we rest in the assurance of it. We thank You for it. Amen.

Active Faith

**Now as you excel in everything—
in faith, in speech, in knowledge, in utmost eagerness,
and in our love for you—
so we want you to excel also in this generous undertaking.**

2 CORINTHIANS 8:7 NRSV

Dear Secret Pal,

Do you desire, as I do, to grow in faith? Like a regularly exercised muscle, our faith will grow and become stronger when we put it into action. But if we allow our faith to become passive and inactive, it will quickly grow weak and dull. It will deteriorate over time.

By keeping our daily relationship with God vibrant, our faith motivates us toward life-changing, miraculous actions. It enables us to reach out to others with grace and love, to pray fervently with lasting results, and to help those in need. It stabilizes our walk with God. Basically, our faith in action allows others to see God's power and glory at work in our lives.

O mighty God, ignite our faith with Your loving fire. Show us areas of our lives where we need to activate our faith. Thank You for Your faithfulness to us. Amen.

Fruitful Prayers

Ask and it will be given you;
seek and you will find;
knock and it will be opened to you.

MATTHEW 7:7 MLB

ᴄᴏ⓪ᴄ⃝ᴏ

Dear Secret Pal,

Prayer, like faith, can easily become passive. It can degenerate to little more than routine mutterings that mean nothing to us, and even less to God. Yet we continue, as if the habit alone is enough to win God's ear. But think about it, we are talking to the Lord of the universe—how dare we step into His presence and mumble something we might not even care about!

First, let's ask for His forgiveness for our foolishness. Then let's reevaluate the real power of prayer. Jesus tells us "to ask, to seek, to knock," making it clear that God waits, ready to listen and answer. So let's begin to pray with honest hearts and thoughtful minds. Let's saturate our prayers with faith, believing that when we ask, we'll receive.

———————— ᴄᴏ⓪ᴄ⃝ᴏ ————————

O Most High, forgive us for taking Your Holy presence for granted. Help us take prayer seriously, approach You in truth and sincerity, and pray the prayer of faith. Amen.

Sanctuary

**Be merciful to me, O God, be merciful to me,
for in you my soul takes refuge;
in the shadow of your wings I will take refuge,
until the destroying storms pass by.**

PSALM 57:1 NRSV

eɔⓈⓄⓈɔ

Dear Secret Pal,

Do you remember where you felt most safe during your childhood? Where did you run after a bad dream or when something went bump in the night? Did you seek shelter beneath the big, fluffy quilt on your mother's bed? Or was it in the secure embrace of your father's comforting arms? We can all relate to that need; and even as grownups, we still long for refuge from time to time.

When those feelings arise, remember we can run to God, dear friend. For He is always ready and waiting to gather us into His arms, to show us mercy and comfort. He longs to protect us from our terrors in the night and send us joyfully on our way!

———————— eɔⓈⓄⓈɔ ————————

Blessed Redeemer, we praise You for making us holy. Sanctify our hearts in Your truth. Amen.

Our Corner of the World

You are the light of the world.
A city built on a hill cannot be hidden. . . . Let your
light shine among the people, so that they observe your
good works and give glory to your heavenly Father.

MATTHEW 5:14,16 MLB

❧

Dear Secret Pal,

How can we make a difference in the world? It's so enormous, and we're so minute—how will our presence ever be noticed? Well, have you ever been in a darkened room where every cubic inch is pitch-black and you can't even see your hand in front of your face? Then someone turns on a small light. In an instant, the darkness flees.

So it is with our faith. It is like a light in a dark world. We need only let it shine, for its effect will be noticed. Sure, we may not be able to reach into all the dark corners of the world, but we can light up the dark corners in our immediate vicinity. We can enlighten those near us: our family, neighbors, friends, and coworkers.

❧

Lord of light, let us shine brightly before others so they might see Your glory and lift their eyes to You. Amen

Miracles

***May miracles and wonders be done
by the name of your holy servant Jesus.***

ACTS 4:30 TLB

Dear Secret Pal,

There are miracles and then there are miracles, like the first crocus of spring, bravely thrusting its way through the ice-cold earth, the glory of the sunrise that chases the dark night, or those first startling cries of a newborn baby facing the world for the first time. These, without doubt, are true and perfect miracles—each one valuable and precious in its own way.

But there are also those miracles that are born of faith, like when someone turns to God for the first time or a lame woman walks. These amazing and life-altering miracles are the result of our partnership with God. When we take a stance of faith and join hands with God, incredible things begin to happen. Some of them are truly miracles!

O mighty God, increase our faith and help us expect miracles, both large and small. Teach us to pray according to Your will and believe that You can do anything! Amen.

Forbearance

Love suffers long and is kind; . . . rejoices
in the truth; bears all things, believes all things,
hopes all things, endures all things.

1 CORINTHIANS 13:4,6-7 NKJV

Dear Secret Pal,

When you truly love someone with your whole heart, you can often endure difficulties that might otherwise overwhelm you. In the dead of night, for instance, a mother willingly rises from the comfort of her bed to help her crying child. Or a wife willingly sets aside her own agenda to listen to her husband tell of his troubles at work. Like a suit of armor, love empowers us to forbear and withstand the challenges that cross our paths.

God's love is no different. His heart tenderly reaches out to us when we are hurting or confused. He expects us to follow His example when our patience is pushed to the limit or we are treated badly. Don't worry; He is always willing to help us by filling us with His perfect love.

Dear blessed Redeemer, You endured so much for us—even to the point of death on the cross. Fill us with Your perfect love that we might practice forbearance with those You have placed around us. Amen.

Sharing

**It is possible to give away and become richer!
It is also possible to hold on too tightly and lose everything.**

PROVERBS 11:24 TLB

ᴄᴏ◎ᴏᴠ

Dear Secret Pal,

Sharing is not a natural human quality. The smallest of children learn to say, "Mine!" Even mature adults struggle with generosity. It's not always easy when someone asks us to share our time, home, talent, or money. In fact, we can come up with many reasons why we should politely decline.

But consider for a moment, all we are has been handed to us by God— on loan, actually, for the duration of our lifetime here on earth. And His purpose for giving to us so generously is that we might imitate His benevolent goodness and give in return. God places us in a position to bless others with our abundance, and then, amazingly, He blesses us even more when we obey. How can we lose?

———————— ᴄᴏ◎ᴏᴠ ————————

Gracious Father, make our hearts more like Yours—always looking for ways to share with others. Teach us to give cheerfully—and then see what You can do! Amen.

How to Change the World

You are the salt of the earth;
but if salt has lost its taste, how can its saltiness be restored? . . .
You are the light of the world.
A city built on a hill cannot be hid.

MATTHEW 5:13-14 NRSV

∽⊙⊙∾

Dear Secret Pal,

*D*o you ever wonder how your life might impact others? Do you hope that your presence in this world might affect those around you for the better? Sometimes when you see people living lives that seem flat and dull and almost hopeless, don't you wish that you could make a difference? That's exactly what being "salt" is all about.

Salt is used to flavor and preserve food. Without salt, food would be bland and tasteless. When we allow God to make us into "salt," our words and actions add a wonderful flavor of love and grace. And we also help preserve values, as we openly live out our relationship with God before the eyes of others.

——————— ∽⊙⊙∾ ———————

*L*ord God, we long to be like a good, savory "salt" to those around us. Let our words and actions stand out like a tasty flavoring to every life with which we come in contact. Amen.

Hospitality

For I was hungry and you gave Me food;
I was thirsty and you gave Me drink;
I was a stranger and you took Me in.

MATTHEW 25:35 NKJV

ᴄᴏ⑥ʘᴏ

Dear Secret Pal,

Hospitality. Even the word can overwhelm us, especially when we are working hard, shuttling children, and maintaining busy households. Usually our reluctance comes from the mistaken notion that we must put together some complicated affair that takes weeks of planning, hours of preparation, and days of cleaning up afterward. You see, though, that's not hospitality at all; that's entertaining.

Hospitality is an openness of heart and home, a willingness to bring in another and share from your abundance. It need be neither fancy nor formal, but love should be the motivation. And the best form of hospitality is the kind that cannot be repaid. When we welcome into our homes those who are unable to return the favor, God says we will be richly blessed in return.

ᴄᴏ⑥ʘᴏ

Dear Father, show us opportunities to extend the warm, friendly hand of hospitality to others. Amen.

God's Correction

**Do not resent it when God chastens and corrects you,
for his punishment is proof of his love.**

PROVERBS 3:11 TLB

೨ⓒⓖ⌇

Dear Secret Pal,

*B*y nature, we do not usually enjoy the process of being corrected, whether by an ill-tempered supervisor or an impatient spouse. Even the memory of a rebuke by a stern-faced teacher can be most unpleasant. The thought of correction is not usually a happy one. But the correction of God is not like that.

When God corrects us, His motivation is purely one of love. His correction is usually gentle and uplifting. To correct us, He can use life's circumstances, a quiet personal conviction of the heart, a section of meaningful Scripture, or the words of a trusted friend. He corrects us because He dearly loves us and wants to see us change and grow and glorify Him.

*D*ear Lord, we come before You in honest humility, praying that You will correct us when we need it, and that we will respond with a teachable spirit. Amen.

Seeking God

*You shall walk after the LORD your God and fear Him,
and keep His commandments and obey His voice;
you shall serve Him and hold fast to Him.*

DEUTERONOMY 13:4 NKJV

ᘓᗧᘚ

Dear Secret Pal,

There are many levels on which our relationships are built. With some individuals we are no more than acquaintances, sharing an occasional greeting. With others we are casual friends who speak once in a while. There are also close friends with whom we regularly share our lives. The rarest of all relationships, however, are those that include a deep commitment of the heart and true intimacy.

There are many different levels of relationship with God also. Some are barely acquainted with Him; others seek Him out when there is trouble in their lives. Some have strong relationships with Him that involve daily fellowship. But God longs for us to know Him in the deepest possible way. How much do you value your relationship with Him, dear friend?

ᘓᗧᘚ

Dear Lover of our souls, increase our love for You. Show us how we can seek You with our whole heart. Teach us to hold fast to You. Amen.

Comfort

You, who have shown me great and severe troubles,
Shall revive me again,
And bring me up again from the depths of the earth.
You shall increase my greatness,
And comfort me on every side.

PSALM 71:20-21 NKJV

Dear Secret Pal,

*W*e all need comfort occasionally, whether it's because we've lost a loved one or simply had a bad day. Ironically, it's often the times when we most need comfort that we push God and others away. Grief and despair can pull us into ourselves. It's a self-defensive position we mistakenly suppose will protect us from more heartache and pain.

We must choose to receive God's comfort, opening our hearts and allowing Him to wrap His arms around us. And then we can rest in His comfort, knowing that He is in control and heals the brokenhearted. He replaces our sadness with joy and will dry our tears. When we learn to accept God's comfort in this manner, we also learn how to comfort others.

*D*ear Lord, we give thanks to You, our Comforter, and remember that only Your loving touch can heal our hearts. Amen.

Meekness

Who is wise and understanding among you?
Show by your good life that your works are done
with gentleness born of wisdom.

JAMES 3:13 NRSV

Dear Secret Pal,

Just because meekness rhymes with weakness doesn't mean the two actually have anything in common. Meekness can be compared to a powerful ox under harness that obediently performs a task of great strength. Although the big ox is obviously strong enough to break out of the harness and run freely, it chooses to remain obedient to its task. That is the picture of meekness.

So it is with us. Although we serve God, He has not enslaved us. We still have the power and strength to say and do all sorts of things—things that could be harmful and destructive. But when we choose to follow God's lead, we display true meekness. And that, dear friend, is a good thing.

Almighty and powerful God, help us submit our strong will to Yours. We know You lead us in the way that is best. Amen.

Reciprocity

**Whatever measure you use to give—large or small—
will be used to measure what is given back to you.**

LUKE 6:38 TLB

⌒⌒

Dear Secret Pal,

*C*an you think of a way to outgive God? Consider all that He has given us—majestic mountains and breathtaking sunsets, lush green fields and towering trees, raging rivers and thundering oceans. And that's just the beginning. He has blessed us with family and friends, food and clothing, places to live, all above and beyond what we need simply to survive. God is very generous!

Our generosity pales next to His, yet He invites us to try. He challenges us to give generously and promises us that we shall also receive—and not just a little. No, God promises to give back in overflowing measure. When we give liberally, He promises to use the same measure with us, so that we can fully understand what it means to give with joy!

———— ⌒⌒ ————

*M*ost generous Lord, we know that our giving stems from a trust relationship with You. Please, help us understand that You are our Provider and that we cannot outgive You. Amen.

Charity

**Take heed that you do not do your charitable deeds
before men, to be seen by them.
Otherwise you have no reward from your Father in heaven.**

MATTHEW 6:1 NKJV

Dear Secret Pal,

God must be delighted to see His children actively helping others.
There is such disparity in the world. Imagine how pleased He must be
when He witnesses our generosity toward others in need. His father's heart
must glow with pride as He watches us share what He's given with those
who have so little.

How wonderful that we have the ability to delight our Heavenly Father
by simply embracing a charitable spirit toward others—especially when we
learn to do so with quiet discretion, not wanting to be observed, and
expecting nothing in return for our labors. For that is when we become like
Him and bring joy to His heart.

Lord God, my secret pal and I wish to please You by living
charitably with those around us. Give us eyes to see the needs of others
and the ability to give with quiet humility. Amen.

Courage

**Do not fear, for I am with you,
do not be afraid, for I am your God;
I will strengthen you, I will help you,
I will uphold you with my victorious right hand.**

ISAIAH 41:10 NRSV

ᘓᘓᘔᘔ

Dear Secret Pal,

*W*hether we admit it or not, we all get frightened occasionally. Sometimes our fears are based on actual danger, and other times they're simply imagined. But when our pulse begins to race and our heart starts to pound, our fears, factual or imagined, feel very real. That means it's time to turn to God.

God is ever ready to deliver us from both our fears and whatever it is that threatens our safety. He promises to stay by our side and strengthen us. Believing His promise is where trust is born. It's easy to believe He upholds us with His victorious right hand.

ᘓᘓᘔᘔ

O mighty God, we know we are fearful creatures. But You promise to strengthen and deliver us. Teach us to call out to You in faith when we come face to face with our fears. Amen.

Surrendering to God's Will

I am waiting for the LORD; my soul is
in expectation, and in His word do I hope.
My soul is looking for the LORD
more than watchmen for the morning.

PSALM 130:5-6 MLB

∾⊙⊙∾

Dear Secret Pal,

To surrender to God's will is to embrace a willingness to wait, for God reveals His will to us in a slow and deliberate way. He hands us one precious, little jigsaw-puzzle piece at a time. Sometimes we wait for years before He gives us a particular piece. While this all requires an infinite amount of patience, if we ask for help, God will provide.

This isn't to suggest that surrendering our wills to God is a dreary process, with long, drawn-out delays, where we sit around waiting for something to happen. Not at all! In fact, a fresh, new discovery lies in each day, even while we are waiting. And in the end, dear friend, the complete picture is well worth waiting for.

∾⊙⊙∾

Dear Lord, help us trust in Your plan and faithful revelation of that plan to our hearts as we wait patiently for You to put each piece into place. Amen.

Fellowship

**This is what I have asked of God for you:
that you will be encouraged and knit together
by strong ties of love,
and that you will have the rich experience of knowing Christ
with real certainty and clear understanding.**

COLOSSIANS 2:2 TLB

⌇⊚⌇

Dear Secret Pal,

You are a gift from God to me—one of the most delightful and satisfying gifts that God can give! Knowing true fellowship with God's children is a sweet taste of His goodness here on earth.

It's too bad that we often deny ourselves this pleasure simply because we are too busy or tired. For fellowship with others allows us to see commonalities and share triumphs and heartaches. In those times, our hearts are wonderfully knit together, leaving us refreshed, encouraged, and uplifted, ready to face life's next challenge. Let's remember to fellowship often, dear friend. It's an important part of God's plan.

⌇⊚⌇

Our Father, remind us of how You love to see Your children enjoying fellowship with each other. Show us ways that we can incorporate true fellowship into our lives on a regular basis. Amen.

Worship

**You are worthy, our Lord and God,
to receive glory and honor and power,
for you created all things.**

REVELATION 4:11 NRSV

Dear Secret Pal,

We are designed to worship. Our spirits crave opportunities to praise our God and King. He made us. To resist worshiping our Creator is similar to capping a bubbling water fountain—everything all around will soon grow dry and parched and shriveled; meanwhile, on the inside, pressure will increase until it reaches explosive levels.

How much better to allow our fountain of praises to flow freely. There are many "unexpected" moments throughout our day to worship our God. We can praise Him for the new day as we go through our morning routine; we can praise Him for His goodness to us as we drive; we can worship in silent reverence while in the workplace; we can enjoy a quiet moment of worship before drifting off to sleep.

All glory to You, Most High! Show us new ways to express our worship and praise to You throughout the course of our day. Amen.

Our Awesome God

But I will sing of Your power;
Yes, I will sing aloud of Your mercy in the morning;
For You have been my defense
And refuge in the day of trouble.

PSALM 59:16 NKJV

Dear Secret Pal,

Our God is awesome beyond our comprehension—the epitome of truth and righteousness. He is perfect, holy, and just, and yet He is simultaneously forgiving, merciful, and kind. How can we fully know the height, depth, and width of His mighty power and everlasting love? Even if we read the entire Bible over and over, we could barely comprehend how amazing our God truly is. It's just too much for our finite minds.

Can you count the grains of sand on a beach or how many times the waves break upon the shore? Neither can we totally understand who God really is. Here on earth, we can know only in part. But one day we shall see Him face to face, my friend, and, oh, what a day that will be!

Our awesome God, we see just a sliver of Your glory and are utterly dumbfounded. Help us offer You honor and respect worthy of Your glory. Amen.

Nothing Is Impossible

**Jesus looked at them intently, then said,
"Without God, it is utterly impossible.
But with God everything is possible."**

MARK 10:27 TLB

୧୬୦

Dear Secret Pal,

*W*ith our God nothing is impossible. And yet we sometimes forget that He actually created the vast universe. He is mighty and powerful and can do any and all things. Nothing is bigger than God—not even the biggest problem in our lives. You can believe me when I tell you that there is no problem too big for God to handle and no circumstance too difficult for Him to solve.

What can you possibly suggest that God's power and strength can't conquer? What seems impossible to us is nothing to Him. Even if we laid every impossibility at His feet, God would not be intimidated. For Him, there's no such thing as impossible!

୧୬୦

*M*ighty God, help us understand that nothing is too great for You. Remind us of Your power and strength and of how You easily conquer the impossible. Amen.

Trusting Him

Trust in the LORD with all your heart,
And lean not on your own understanding;
In all your ways acknowledge Him,
And He shall direct your paths.

PROVERBS 3:5-6 NKJV

Dear Secret Pal,

Trust. It should be an easy thing. Just sit back, relax, rely on God to take care of you. Yet it's never that simple, is it? When we place our lives in God's hands, it is a wonderful feeling of relief and release. But sooner or later, the storms of life begin to challenge our confidence. And then suddenly, thinking we can handle life on our own, we're ready to leap out of God's hands.

Fortunately, God can easily reach out and still the raging seas. And those stormy times serve as new opportunities to trust Him. The more rough seas we encounter with Him, the more we begin to realize that He really is in control and that we can trust Him in all areas of our lives.

Heavenly Father, we offer You our quietly trusting hearts,
believing in Your promise to deliver us and to direct our paths. Amen.

God's Sovereignty

**Then the seventh angel blew his trumpet,
and there were loud voices in heaven, saying,
"The kingdom of the world has become
the kingdom of our Lord and of his Messiah,
and he will reign forever and ever."**

REVELATION 11:15 NRSV

꩜

Dear Secret Pal,

*O*ne day we will all gather in joyous celebration before the throne of almighty God and proclaim Him "King of kings, Lord of lords, Ruler of the universe." His kingdom and sovereignty will be made known to the ends of the heavens and the earth, and every knee shall bow down to honor Him.

But even before that grand moment when God is proclaimed Lord of all, we can proclaim Him King of our hearts. We can bow down and honor Him. We can serve Him with eager hearts. And when we do, we will begin to experience the pleasures and rewards of God's kingdom here on earth.

꩜

*M*ighty King, teach us to honor and exalt You during the ordinary moments of our daily lives so that we might experience Your kingdom and authority here on earth. Amen.

God's Timing

**Wait for the LORD; take courage,
and He will give strength to your heart;
yes, wait for the LORD.**

PSALM 27:14 MLB

Dear Secret Pal,

We measure time in earthly ways, carefully counting hours, days, years, and we take these measurements quite seriously. But God, who is eternal and perfect, doesn't rely on such methods. His timing is flawless. He moves when it's right to move, and He acts when all is in place and ready—not a moment too soon, not a second too late. And all this He does without the help of a clock or calendar!

So how do we adjust ourselves to God's timing? Living in the world, we can't exactly throw away our datebooks and alarm clocks. Yet if we can trust that His timing is perfect, and rest assured that He hears our prayers and will answer accordingly, we might begin to understand eternity.

Dear Father, help us recognize that You measure time differently than we do. Open our hearts and minds to accept that Your timing is far better than ours. Amen.

Our Confidence

In God's presence I have such confidence through Christ
not because we possess self-sufficiency to regard anything as
from ourselves, but because our sufficiency is God-given.

2 CORINTHIANS 3:4-5 MLB

Dear Secret Pal,

*D*on't we all long for confidence—to walk into a room with head held high, exuding assurance with each step? But such confidence often eludes us because we attach it to things like appearance, wealth, or social status. However, that sort of confidence is a thin veneer that can be easily chipped to reveal the flawed and imperfect human beneath.

Real and lasting confidence is heart-deep and richly satisfying. It comes from our relationship with God. Having been forgiven and received by our Heavenly Father, we can hold our heads up without shame; and we can be assured that, in Him, we are being made whole and complete. His grace is sufficient; He's all we need. Thus can we stride through life with perfect confidence.

*F*ather God, we look to You for confidence that is rooted deeply in our hearts, allowing us to move through our daily lives with our heads held high—because of You! Amen.

Growing

**I am confident of this:
that the One who has begun his good work in you
will go on developing it until the day of Jesus Christ.**

PHILIPPIANS 1:6 PHILLIPS

Dear Secret Pal,

We are "works in progress," not yet complete. Like an oil painting, with pigment still wet, we remain under the Master's artful brush, in constant development—a shade here, a tint there, a swirl, an angle, a new perspective. But it can be challenging to be in process. It's easy to become impatient with ourselves and what might seem the sluggish pace of our progress. Yet that is not what God desires.

Because He has designed us each uniquely, He helps us grow and develop individually. This doesn't happen overnight. But if we remain in fellowship with Him, submitting to His touch, we'll continue to grow and change, getting better every day.

Heavenly Father, help us trust and submit to Your perfect brush strokes upon our lives, knowing that only You know what we are to become. Amen.

God's Vessels of Love

**This is My command,
that you love one another
as I have loved you.**

JOHN 15:12 MLB

☙◎ॐ

Dear Secret Pal,

God pours infinite quantities of His love into this world every single day. And He uses us—His human vessels—to do it. That's right. We are His instruments of love to the world.

Like vessels, we are empty inside—until He fills us with Himself and His love. But God has much more in mind than simply filling us. He also wants to use us to pour out onto others the love He's given us. As we pour out God's love, generously and with grace, He fills us again and again! So instead of clutching His love as if it's the last drop, we should allow it to flow freely through us—always clean and fresh and pure!

☙◎ॐ

Dear Lover of our souls, fill us anew with Your love that we might enjoy its freshness, and then pour it out onto others. Remind us of the health benefits of this consistent flow as we position ourselves to be constantly filled by You. Amen.

Fruit of the Spirit

The fruit of the Spirit is love, joy, peace,
longsuffering, kindness, goodness,
faithfulness, gentleness, self-control.
Against such there is no law.

GALATIANS 5:22-23 NKJV

Dear Secret Pal,

*O*nly a mature and healthy tree can bear high-quality fruit. And so it is with us as we grow in the Lord. When we sink our roots deeply into Him, extend our branches upward toward the light of His grace, and drink in the water of love, we begin to bear fruit.

The spiritual fruit we bear is pure and selfless love, deep-flowing joy, quiet peace, goodness, kindness, gentleness, and, finally, self-control that rules the heart. Though highly desirable, this fruit cannot become our goal. For like a tree, we must focus our energies on growth, with roots planted deeply in God, as we drink of His love and grace. For that's when fruit appears, a natural result of our relationship with Him.

*D*ear Lord, teach us to be like a tree rooted firmly in You. Let us look to You. Then we will rejoice when You bear fruit in us. Amen.

Our Earthly Shells

**Glorify God in your body, and
in your spirit, which are God's.**

1 CORINTHIANS 6:20 KJV

Dear Secret Pal,

We sometimes forget that God designed everything about us—even our physical bodies. And occasionally we might even take these "earth-suits" for granted, knowing that they are only temporary and will one day pass away. Or perhaps we take the other extreme, exalting youth and health, expending much time and energy to preserve them.

But neither of these lifestyles glorifies God. He considers our bodies to be like a temple to house His Holy Spirit within us. Being a temple suggests the need for proper care and regular maintenance to keep our bodies in the best possible condition. While that doesn't mean we worship our temples or elevate them above God, it does mean that we treat them with dignity and respect. In so doing, we glorify God.

Wonderful Father, help us understand that our bodies are Your temples. We want to please You in the way we treat them. Amen.

The Unforeseen

Why are you cast down, O my soul?
And why are you disquieted within me?
Hope in God, for I shall yet praise Him
For the help of His countenance.

PSALM 42:5 NKJV

Dear Secret Pal,

Sometimes things happen. Things we don't expect. Things we never dreamed could occur in our lives. At these times, we naturally want to ask "why?" We should be thankful, dear friend, that we don't know the future (good or bad). For such knowledge would alter our lives completely. Instead we must learn that the unexpected will happen—as inevitably as the rain.

The good news is that we have someone to see us through these troubling times. Our Source of hope is greater than any unforeseen event, and we can trust that He will not allow us to be destroyed. Whatever catastrophic event might occur, it is not bigger than God. He will strengthen and deliver us.

Precious Lord, help ground our hearts in You so when hard times arise, we will not be shaken. Increase our faith so our strength in You might encourage others. Amen.

A Found Life

He who finds his life will lose it,
and he who loses his life for My sake will find it.
He who receives you receives Me, and
he who receives Me receives Him who sent Me.

MATTHEW 10:39-40 NKJV

Dear Secret Pal,

Have you ever asked "Why am I here?" Many people spend their whole lives trying to answer that question. The human soul hungers for fulfillment and self-understanding. But all this self-seeking is as futile as a puppy chasing his own tail.

Our answers come when we step outside our shallow little lives and turn our eyes toward God, seeking Him with earnestness and truth. For when we find Him, He begins to reveal to us the purpose for our lives. We see that we are who we are for good reason. We realize that in finding God we have found ourselves!

Precious Lord, teach our hearts to seek You. And when we find You, help us see ourselves for what You have made us, and then help us live according to Your divine plan. Amen.

Like Little Children

Truly I tell you,
whoever does not receive the kingdom of God
as a little child will never enter it.

MARK 10:15 NRSV

Dear Secret Pal,

We can become so caught up in being mature and responsible that we nearly forget we once were children. Can you remember how it felt to be young and carefree—romping barefoot through the grass on a summer morning? As adults we often forget the sweet, trusting innocence of childhood.

God encourages us to become, once again, like little children—to take Him literally at His Word, to believe without doubt His amazing promises. The wise of this world cannot understand such childlike faith. They rationalize and dispute God's power and majesty. But let's exchange our skeptical adult ways for childlike faith and see if we don't experience God with freshness and life!

---

*O*ur Heavenly Father, we come before You as little children, You are our Daddy. We joyfully trust and believe that You can do all things! Amen.

God's Gifts

**Every beneficent gift
and every perfect present is from above;
it descends from the Father of lights.**

JAMES 1:17 MLB

Dear Secret Pal,

We will never fully understand or appreciate God's ability to give good and perfect gifts. But we glimpse His goodness by witnessing His amazing creation—beautiful trees, fragrant flowers, singing birds, and so much more! And that's just the beginning of His gifts.

He has given us health and family and friends and generous provisions, and so much more for which to be thankful! And still that is not all. He gives us spiritual gifts and encouragement and strength. He also holds for us a gift of eternity and an everlasting kingdom where we can dwell in His presence forever. And all of these wonderful gifts are a direct result of His greatest gift ever, His Son. What a wonderful God we serve!

Generous and loving Father, we thank You for all the gifts You have given. We are amazed by Your kind and generous heart. Help us learn from You and be giving, too. Amen.

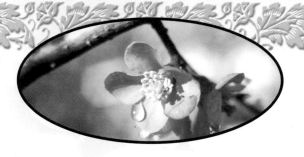

God, the Creator

Have you not known?
Have you not heard?
The everlasting God, the LORD,
The Creator of the ends of the earth.

ISAIAH 40:28 NKJV

꿈ᄀᄀᄀ

Dear Secret Pal,

One of God's greatest love letters to the world is written in the form of His beautiful creation. Consider majestic mountains, voluminous canyons, dense rain forests, or the ocean depths, and be utterly amazed. Or consider a flower blossom or snowflake—perfect, yet impossible to reproduce.

How can we not be awestruck when we consider these things? How can we honestly look at any part of God's magnificent creation and walk away unchanged? My heart longs to embrace His creation as a sweet letter of love. Join with me, dear friend, and let's determine to open and read it in fresh awareness each new day.

Awesome Creator, we see Your words of love written across a colorful sunset or Your strength magnified in the glory of a thunderstorm. We rejoice in Your creation. Amen.

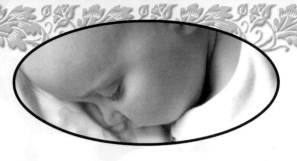

Rest

Come to me and I will give you rest—
all of you who work so hard beneath a heavy yoke.
Wear my yoke—for it fits perfectly—and let me teach you;
for I am gentle and humble, and you shall find rest for your
souls; for I give you only light burdens.

MATTHEW 11:28-30 TLB

Dear Secret Pal,

*S*ometimes it seems we plod along beneath a heavy burden, day-in, day-out, carrying an unwieldy load that saps our energy and erodes our strength. As we shoulder our responsibilities and trudge along, we find ourselves longing for rest, real rest.

That's when God reaches out to our hearts and says, "Come to me, and I will give you rest." As we let Him, He gently removes the heavy and ill-fitting yoke that we've mistakenly placed upon ourselves and replaces it with one that's light and flexible, perfectly fitted to our lives.

*D*ear Lord Jesus, we long for the rest that You can bring to our lives. We place our trust in You. Thank You for helping us to enter into Your rest. Amen.

Fulfillment

**For he satisfies the thirsty,
and the hungry he fills with good things.**

PSALM 107:9 NRSV

◦◦◦◦

Dear Secret Pal,

*F*rom the moment of birth, we begin our search for fulfillment. For this is how we were designed to operate as humans. We start out simply, seeking satisfaction for our basic needs of food and drink, warmth and rest. As we grow and mature, we begin to sense another longing—one that we try to fill with many things —until finally, we realize that what we truly need is God.

When we give our lives to God, we realize that we are complete only in Him. Only He can answer our needs and satisfy our hearts. We must go to Him. Whenever that feeling of unrest stirs in us, that longing for fulfillment, we must remember to continue to seek Him. He alone can fill us.

─────────── ◦◦◦◦ ───────────

*G*lorious Provider, we come to You now and ask You to fill our hearts. We acknowledge that only You can bring the fulfillment for which we long. Please fill us again. Amen.

Discerning God's Will

**When the Spirit of truth comes,
he will guide you into all the truth.**

JOHN 16:13 NRSV

Dear Secret Pal,

How can we know God's purpose for our lives? We long to make decisions that are wise and sound, and yet so often we feel uncertain about which direction to go. If only God would write us a message across the sky in brilliant, uppercase letters.

But God seems to prefer to let us discover His plan gradually as we come to know Him better. As we live life, we learn to hear His soft voice speaking to our hearts and urging us in the direction we should go. Like working a jigsaw puzzle, He gives us one piece at a time. The pieces may not seem like much taken one by one, but as each finds its place alongside the others, the picture emerges. He will surely reveal His plan, one piece at a time.

Dear Father, give us patience to see Your plan and purpose for our lives emerging as we are faithful to place the pieces together as You direct—one piece at a time. Amen.

Angels

For He gives His angels orders regarding you,
to protect you wherever you go.
They will support you with their hands
lest you strike your foot against a stone.

PSALM 91:11-12 MLB

Dear Secret Pal,

*A*ngels are popular these days, and according to the Bible they are real spiritual beings that do exist. But have you ever wondered if angels are really at work in your life? Do they stand winged guard at your back and side the way masterpiece and contemporary paintings depict them? Or do we, unawares, meet them in their human guise?

Most often in biblical accounts, they were messengers from God that sometimes offered help and protection. It seems quite likely that God still sends angels today. But whether we are protected by angels or by God's own hand, we can be assured that we will always remain safe in His care.

*A*lmighty God, thank You for angels and their work here on earth. While we don't place our faith in them, we do thank You for the many ways You have created to ensure our safety. Amen.

Freedom from Want

Don't worry at all about having enough food and clothing....
Your heavenly Father already knows perfectly well
that you need them.

MATTHEW 6:31-32 TLB

Dear Secret Pal,

It's not unusual to carry ways of thinking from our childhood into our adulthood, often without conscious realization. But these nearly forgotten memories can impair the way we serve and trust God. For instance, if as children we felt our physical and emotional needs weren't always met, we may as adults question whether God can, or will, meet our needs today.

To completely trust God, we must release our childhood memories and acknowledge that God can care for us as can no other. He knows how and when to give us exactly what we need. And when we trust Him, we will become miraculously free from want.

O Lord, our Provider, thank You for giving us all we need. Transform our minds to trust You implicitly and to free us from want. Amen.

Visiting the Sick

**Inasmuch as you did it to one of the least
of these My brethren, you did it to Me.**

MATTHEW 25:40 NKJV

⌒⊚⊙⌒

Dear Secret Pal,

*A*s our lives are steadily transformed by the loving influence of our gracious God, our hearts long to reach out to others. We want to touch those whose hearts are troubled, whose lives are in turmoil, whose health and life may be hanging in the balance.

We want to reach out to the sick — to visit them, to pray for them, and to offer encouragement. And soon we realize that doing this for others is like doing it for God Himself. Parents can understand this analogy, for if their child is in need and someone helps him or her, it's as if they have been helped as well. So, dear friend, let's become more like Him, learning to reach out to those who are sick.

⌒⊚⊙⌒

*G*reat Physician, make our hearts more like Yours, and teach us to recognize others who need Your touch. Make us willing to become Your hands of mercy. Amen.

Faith in the Unseen

**Now faith is the assurance of things hoped for,
the conviction of things not seen.**

HEBREWS 11:1 NRSV

Dear Secret Pal,

It's always a challenge to walk in faith. Life presents many opportunities to "believe only what we see." But God has called us to faith in Him, dear friend. He has invited us to walk among what's unseen and yet to believe. And though it's not always an easy journey, it is always fulfilling.

When we choose to put our faith in God and trust Him to help us, even though our heads tell us it's impossible, we are choosing to walk by faith. Faith is not based upon things we can explain or even see with our own eyes. Faith is based upon the belief that nothing is impossible for Him. Faith will lead us right into His glorious presence.

All-powerful God, thank You for Your gift of faith. Teach us to hope in Your unseen promises, Lord, and to walk steadfastly in faith. Amen.

Our Connection

I am the Vine, you are the branches.
He who remains in Me, and I in him, bears much fruit.
For apart from Me you can do nothing.

JOHN 15:5 MLB

Dear Secret Pal,

It's wonderfully reassuring and comforting to know that we are connected to God. He describes Himself as the vine and us as the branches that stem from that vine. He then explains how this relationship bonds us together as one. The vine nourishes the branches, infusing us with His life force. What a comforting thought!

If the branches remain tightly connected, allowing moisture and nutrition to flow through the vine into them, they will stay healthy and even bear fruit! So it is with us, dear friend. As we remain connected to our Lord, we will also live healthy and fruitful lives. Such a simple example—yet so profound!

Precious Lord, how we long for connection. Please help us remain so tightly connected to You that Your life might flow through us and bless many. Amen.

Doing Good

**Do not neglect to do good
and to share what you have,
for such sacrifices are pleasing to God.**

HEBREWS 13:16 NRSV

ভ⊚ট

Dear Secret Pal,

*A*nother result of loving and serving God is that our hearts are transformed and made more like our Heavenly Father's. As His characteristics become established in our lives, we begin to look for ways to please and imitate Him. We long to do good for others, just as He has done good things for us.

We might be amazed if we realized how many people need a helping hand—and even more amazed to realize how much we can help. Some people who need help live across the ocean; some live next door. God can always point us in the right direction. And with His help, we can pass along to others the goodness He has freely given us.

ভ⊚ট

*L*oving Father, please show us now who it is that we can help. And show us how we can help that person. Make our hearts more like Yours as we seek out those in need. Amen.

Reaching Out

Go therefore and make disciples of all the nations,
baptizing them in the name of the Father
and the Son and of the Holy Spirit.

MATTHEW 28:19 NKJV

Dear Secret Pal,

Not everyone is able to stand up before a large crowd and preach the gospel. For some of us, such things are truly terrifying. Yet we can all share the good news of God's love in some way.

Since God designed us, He recognizes our different gifts. He knows what we can or cannot do. Often He places us in situations where we can reveal His love to others as we live out our lives. But occasionally God puts us in situations that are more challenging, empowering us to do and say things beyond our normal selves. That can be exciting! But first we must be ready and willing. Only as we listen to Him and respond to His Spirit's gentle nudges, can we share His glory with others.

Dear Lord, give us willing hearts to share Your love with those who have not yet heard. We will listen carefully to Your voice and step out in faith as You present us with opportunities. Amen.

Freedom

**There is therefore now no condemnation
for those who are in Christ Jesus.
For the law of the Spirit of life in Christ Jesus
has set you free from the law of sin and of death.**

ROMANS 8:1-2 NRSV

～⊚∾

Dear Secret Pal,

*W*hen Jesus laid down His life, He freed us to live our lives to the
fullest. That's not to suggest that life in Him is a "free-for-all." Indeed this
new freedom carries some responsibilities with it.

The primary responsibility is to live in love or, in other words, let God's
love rule richly in our lives. When love rules, we discover that freedom
abounds. We are no longer performance-oriented, approval-hungry, law-
bound citizens. Rather we are fellow humans whose motivation is love.
What a difference that makes! When love is behind our deeds and actions,
the results quickly become eternal. When love directs our decisions, the
impact is often life changing. Indeed the law of love truly sets us free!

━━━━━━━ ～⊚∾ ━━━━━━━

*H*eavenly Father, help us embrace freedom and live according to
the law of love. Amen.

A Time for Everything

**To everything there is a season,
A time for every purpose under heaven.**

ECCLESIASTES 3:1 NKJV

Dear Secret Pal,

*L*ife has many seasons. Sometimes we struggle against them, hoping to resist the changes. But just as it is futile for a tree to cling to its colorful leaves when an autumn storm unleashes its fury, so it is ridiculous for us to fight against the seasons of our lives.

Whether we are just starting a spring season where new growth and life are bursting forth from us, or we are in the midst of a dark and dormant winter where it seems all we can do is wait, we need to remember that our lives and times are in God's hands. He has a season for everything. More than that, He has a purpose for each and every season. He knows when we need to be bearing and harvesting fruit, just as He knows when we need to rest quietly. All we need to do is trust Him.

---

*A*ll-knowing God, help us respect the seasons that You bring to our lives. Teach us not to resist change but to celebrate Your hand upon us and to cooperate with Your plan. Amen.

True Joy

For the LORD takes pleasure in His people,
and adorns the humble with salvation.
Let the godly rejoice in this honor;
Let them shout for joy.

PSALM 149:4-5 MLB

⟨⊚⟩

Dear Secret Pal,

*T*rue joy can be found only in the Lord. We can pursue earthly delights and pleasures to the point of sheer exhaustion and still never find joy. But when we come to the Lord in joyful celebration of His glory, we can discover the love and the life that bring our hearts lasting joy.

If you ask people what they most want out of life, many will say, "To be happy." Yet without God, we would all still be looking. That's one reason it's imperative that we allow God's true joy to take deep root in our lives. We want to exude His joy to others wherever we go so they begin to wonder where they might find it, too.

⟨⊚⟩

O wondrous Lord, let me rejoice in Your goodness and mercy, and let Your joy flow through me like a bubbling stream, that others might see it and discover the Source. Amen.

God's Mysterious Plan

He has made known to us the mystery of his will,
according to his good pleasure that he set forth in Christ,
as a plan for the fullness of time.

EPHESIANS 1:9-10 NRSV

Dear Secret Pal,

*G*od's ways are higher than ours, so how can we fully comprehend His great and mysterious plan? While we understand bits and pieces, His plan, in whole, remains a mystery until we see Him face to face.

But we do know this about His plan: Since the beginning of time, He has worked to unite Heaven and earth with Him in perfect love. His goal is to redeem a world that is lost and perishing without Him, to bestow love and grace upon all who would receive it. We partake in this plan, dear friend, when we work as His ambassadors of love and good will, partnering in grace and mercy to unite Heaven and earth for His never-ending glory!

O holy Lord, let us unite with You in Your wonderful and mysterious plan. Let us partner with You as You draw Heaven and earth together by the power of Your never-ending love and grace! Amen.

If you have enjoyed this book, you will also enjoy the Psalms Gift Edition™ series available from your local bookstore.

Lighthouse Psalms
Garden Psalms
Love Psalms
Psalms for Women

If this book has impacted your life, we would like to hear from you.

Please contact us at:

Honor Books
Department E
P.O. Box 55388
Tulsa, Oklahoma 74155

or by e-mail at:
info @ honorbooks.com